Voices from the Front Line

Voices from the Front Line

Ideas to Help Educators Solve Today's Crucial Issues

Edited by Heather Dean
and Amber E. Wagnon

ROWMAN & LITTLEFIELD
Lanham • Boulder • New York • London

Published by Rowman & Littlefield
An imprint of The Rowman & Littlefield Publishing Group, Inc.
4501 Forbes Boulevard, Suite 200, Lanham, Maryland 20706
www.rowman.com

6 Tinworth Street, London SE11 5AL, United Kingdom

Copyright © 2021 by Heather Dean and Amber E. Wagnon

All rights reserved. No part of this book may be reproduced in any form or by any electronic or mechanical means, including information storage and retrieval systems, without written permission from the publisher, except by a reviewer who may quote passages in a review.

British Library Cataloguing in Publication Information Available

Library of Congress Cataloging-in-Publication Data Available

ISBN 978-1-4758-6277-5 (cloth)
ISBN 978-1-4758-6278-2 (pbk.)
ISBN 978-1-4758-6279-9 (electronic)

*To David, my husband and partner for over 25 years.
No matter what I set my mind to, you remain my steadfast cheering section. With you, I will always accomplish more. Thanks for walking by my side on this journey. With all my love, Heather*

*To my husband, Kelly, and our incredible kids, Kayleigh and Pierce.
Thank you three for the constant love and support.
Amber/Mom*

Contents

Preface		ix
Acknowledgments		xi
Introduction		xiii
1	Care Defined, Care Refined *Jolleen de Clercq and Nikkole Swanson*	1
2	Grief in the Classroom *Stephanie Heitkemper*	11
3	Recognizing and Responding to Commercially Sexually Exploited Children *Debbie Johnson and Katherine Grayson*	27
4	Homelessness and the Classroom: Educators Responding with Care *Kourtney Kauffman and Samantha Van Horn*	41
5	Children of the Incarcerated *Nita Brady*	63
6	Becoming a Bodhi-Teacha: Actualizing Antiracist Practices *Amelia Herrera*	75
7	The Newcomer Student Experience: Opportunities to Empower, Engage, and Advocate for Immigrant Students *Lindsey Bird*	95
8	Building Meaningful Student and Parent Relationships *Nicole Lonergan and Ryan Lonergan*	111
9	Games and Play as a Supportive Part of a Pedagogy of Care *Anthony Avery, Kelly B. Binz, and Melissa S. Williams*	129
10	Making Space for Mindfulness *Samantha Houston-Crook*	147
About the Editors and Contributors		161

Preface

Caring was first recognized as a central element of teaching by Nel Noddings in 1984 and again in 2003. She later asserted that caring means a person is willing to "really hear, see, or feel what the other tries to convey" (Noddings, 2005, pp. 15–16). The ideas presented in this definition, of course, are not new to educators. Educators enter the field largely because they already care deeply about students, schools, and community.

However, implementing a pedagogy of care in schools and classrooms is a more difficult concept to conceptualize. In her second edition of *Caring*, Noddings urges her readers to consider the question: Is direct, externally observable action necessary to caring? The editors of this book grappled with this question as well, concluding that a pedagogy of care is first a mindset, then discernable actions. In an effort to demonstrate such a mindset, our previous work presented narratives to highlight the empathy that Noddings argued should be present in educational settings. This new work provides tools that educators can use to inform their practices.

While there are many accounts and much research that substantiates the importance of caring in education, there is less specific guidance on how to foster such relationships and environments. Instead, educators are often given recommendations and information on topics such as classroom supervision and curriculum.

We recognize that the responsibilities educators are tasked with, including instruction and classroom management, are important; but we contend that without an underlining pedagogy of care, the content knowledge will be much less valuable. The experts in this book seek to move past singular narrative examples to offer specific guidance, direction, and strategies to help the reader understand and approach the complex issues their students face.

REFERENCES

Noddings, N. (2003). *Caring: A feminine approach to ethics and moral education* (2nd ed.). University of California Press. (Original work published 1984)

Noddings, N. (2005). *The challenge to care in schools: An alternative approach to education* (2nd ed.). Teachers College Press.

Acknowledgments

We would like to thank all of the authors who contributed to this book. They stepped up to share with passion and dedication what they know to be true as well as what they strive to practice! In the best of times, this is a feat worthy of recognition; however, during the pandemic, this accomplishment deserves an extra round of applause! We hope you can hear us cheering for you!

With much appreciation,
Heather Dean and Amber Wagnon

Introduction

Thank you for opening up *Voices from the Front Line*! We are so glad you have taken the time to learn with us! Education is the greatest of professions as we are constantly in a position to learn, grow, and refine our practices. This book was birthed with this sentiment in mind.

In our 2020 book, *Hear My Voice: Tales of Trauma and Equity from Today's Youth*, many of our colleagues and our teacher education students provided us with valuable insights. While it was clear our readers valued the book's narratives as well as the brain research, many shared that they longed for more practical applications to take into the classroom.

We couldn't agree more! Practice is the heart of teaching. This new book was written to address this need and serve as a companion text to *Hear My Voice*. We hope this book honors your feedback and requests. We have invited those we hold in high esteem to share their area of expertise with you, while providing you with actionable steps you can take into your class the next day.

As you read the chapters that follow, we hope you are able to walk away with a few new tools from each chapter to continue to grow and refine your purpose and pedagogy. Enjoy the journey!

We would love to hear from you. Please share your stories and your journey with us at educatorsinpursuit.com.

All the best,
Heather and Amber

ONE
Care Defined, Care Refined

Jolleen de Clercq and Nikkole Swanson

> No significant learning occurs without a significant relationship.
> —Dr. James Comer

EXPECTED LEARNING OUTCOMES

- Readers will explore various definitions of care.
- Readers will discern how love and sense of belonging are the driving forces behind building a successful and authentic relationship with students.
- Readers will collect strategies to foster and curate relationships and care for students.
- Readers will consider self-care practices and learn how caring for oneself is the cornerstone of care in the classroom.

WHAT WE KNOW

When Jill began teaching, she had a litany of philosophies and ideologies about what type of educator she would become. She grew up surrounded by educators. Her mom was an elementary school teacher, her great-uncle was a Harvard professor, and her grandfather was a county school board president. She presumptuously believed that education ran through her veins and thought of herself as a natural-born teacher. She would simply teach the content, and the students would learn and engage with everything she had to say.

Jill's mindset crashed and burned the minute she walked into her first job as a sixth-grade teacher in an urban elementary school. And while Jill was creative and engaging, she found herself in daily conflicts with her students and their families. Her students were often combative when she would try to address misbehavior. Furthermore, their misconduct never seemed to be remedied when she used the behavior management system she learned in the credential program. This was all compounded by the fact that when she would communicate with parents about the students' misconduct, they were displeased with Jill, not their children.

These persistent issues were not something Jill was prepared to handle. She worked tirelessly on her lesson plans, beautifully decorated her classroom, and perfectly laminated folders. What was causing the disconnect? Why did the students and their parents believe her motives to be insidious? What was Jill missing?

WHAT YOU NEED TO KNOW

There are many definitions of care circulating the world, but the most applicable for this book comes from Carla Shalaby (2020, p. 42), who states that care is "not about being kind or charitable; rather, care is about being and working in ways that are fair, inclusive, and in solidarity with the most vulnerable." Furthermore, caring for students includes building relationships so that students feel love and a sense of belonging in their classroom community.

Every child has a story, which means that we as educators must work to listen, understand, support, and be dependable figures in each student's life. But not all students need the same amount of care. That is caring equally. Equality is a vital practice in education, but a direct path to genuine, equitable care and successful teacher efficacy is to ask yourself, "Do my students know that when they need me to move beyond kindness and charity and provide them with care and sacrifice, I will be that reliable agent of change?"

Abraham Maslow's hierarchy of needs suggests that before educators can expect students to reach their full potential, they must make sure their basic needs are being met (physiological, safety, belonging and love, esteem, and self-actualization). Matthew Lieberman, in contrast, believes that caring adults should begin with belonging and love, and argues that it is relationships that provide us with our physiological needs and safety needs (Sprenger, 2020).

As humans, those in caring professions can relate that to feel a sense of belonging is not only something craved but also a necessary factor in personal and professional growth. Belonging is a key component of inclusion. Teachers can relate to this because they, too, have the desire to feel included. Every day, the perception of acceptance among school leaders and fellow staff members provides educators with a certain level of comfort and motivates them to continue to put in the work, even when circumstances become overwhelmingly challenging.

This level of comfort and belonging also applies to students of all ages and backgrounds. For students to achieve greater success, their perception of truly being an accepted member of the classroom community is essential. Making a student feel the safety, comfort, and reliability of a classroom takes great sacrifice. And when genuine sacrifices are made, the bridge between love and care is amalgamated.

For example, when a student is consistently listless or disengaged, and the teacher reaches out to communicate and elicit reasons why that student is not engaging with the class, the teacher is demonstrating kindness or concern. This is important, but to provide authentic care, the teacher will have to go above and beyond kindness or concern. She will have the conversation with that student, follow up daily, and routinely self-reflect to determine the effectiveness of these conversations.

When the student sees the teacher being consistent, respectful, patient, and present, she or he may gain a sense of belonging and trust, which can naturally lead to love. Love is the foundation needed to help students build their emotional strength; it is fundamental to functioning as a whole child. While there are various forms and degrees of love that can be expressed, love in the classroom is unconditional, equitable, and accepts and validates students for who they are as unique individuals.

Love listens. Love is patient. Love is setting high expectations and truly believing in your core that those expectations can be met. Without love and a sense of belonging, a student will likely reject even what some may consider the best teaching. A child will remember how you made them feel much more than the content taught.

WHAT YOU CAN DO

Work Hard, Care Hard

> Care is hard work because it requires genuine sacrifice, but young children can—and do—welcome hard work.
> —Carla Shalaby

John Hattie studied more than 250 influences on learning outcomes, and the number-one factor that positively affects student achievement is collective teacher efficacy. Teacher efficacy is "the shared belief that through their collective action, educators can positively influence student outcomes, including those who are disengaged and/or disadvantaged" (Hattie, 2016). In other words, the most influential factor in positive student achievement is teachers' attitudes or beliefs about the potential of their students. No other factor impacts a student more than a teacher's mindset. This hopeful truth is an anchor, as the only entity a teacher can control in the classroom is herself.

Even with research on the crucial necessity of teacher efficacy, teachers often find themselves in professional development centered around curriculum and content. And while curriculum and content are a big part of the job, professional development geared toward these topics alone will not profoundly impact student achievement. Therefore, the teacher who makes a lasting impact is the one who seeks out opportunities to educate herself on the crucial aspects of reaching all students, even outside of the school day.

A teacher, with the goal of achieving efficacy, will work to feel competent and confident in her ability to empower all students to succeed. Teacher efficacy requires an immense amount of trust, which must be built over time. The intent is to make the effort to take the reins and change the status quo. But while efficacy is about self-betterment, the development cannot be done alone. The conscious effort to engage in conversations regarding efficacy must be the collective responsibility of all educators and stakeholders.

Care Equally, Care Equitably

> My students don't need me to learn. They need me to care.
> —Liz Galarza

All students deserve to be equally cared about by their school community. But the effort, the specialization, and the individualization of that care—rather than for a whole class—is when authentic care can take place. In most professions, individualized care is necessary to be successful. A physician cannot provide the same care to each of his patients. Nor could a mechanic repair each automobile in the same fashion. The same applies to education. Every child has a story that is unique to their life and needs. Those needs must be addressed in different ways.

Schools have generalized policies that encourage student conformity on how to act and behave. While these rules and policies are important for safety and order, they do not consider a child's background, culture, home life, and experiences. For example, a school site may have a strict policy about bringing Chromebooks to class fully charged. If a student brings a dead Chromebook to class, the teacher takes points off a student's grade. But what if that student is living in a situation with little to no access to electricity? What if their charger is consistently stolen? These types of policies do not instill responsibility. They only perpetuate the achievement gap between the "haves" and the "have nots."

In her influential work, *A Framework for Understanding Poverty* (2003), Dr. Ruby K. Payne introduces the concept of hidden rules of economic class systems and addresses the achievement gap. This work outlines how the salient mores or rules of different class systems function in students' lives. Schools operate with middle-class rules and influences, yet the majority of schools in California are serving children living below the poverty line. School and classroom policies cannot function under equal practices alone. That will leave too many students without the services, safety, and sense of belonging they need to thrive and be successful in the classroom.

Children and young adults will not feel love or a sense of belonging if classrooms, schools, and districts continue to function in the lane of middle-class systems. If educators were to constantly provide *equitable* care, acknowledging differences and diversity among their student population, they will innately model the value of taking care of each other and honoring the community that has been built, driving students to take care of themselves and their peers.

The most direct path to acquiring insight and empathy into students' reality is through building and fostering student–teacher relationships. Building a mutual relationship with students is not for indolent teachers.

Relationships with students take patience, effort, and sacrifice. The secondary school teacher has an especially difficult time curating these relationships because there are many more students on a roster than that of an elementary school teacher. The good news is that all teachers, regardless of what or to whom they are teaching, can integrate strategies that curate positive relationships with students.

One of the best ways to build a relationship is to provide voice and choice. When students decide how they might like to practice a skill or demonstrate a learning goal, they are practicing independent decision-making, and therefore empowering themselves in the classroom environment. When they can reflect on their needs, strengths, and interests, students begin to understand themselves and each other better and will, in turn, be able to form stronger connections to others in the classroom.

Take, for example, a fourth-grade teacher who encourages her students to hone in on how they best demonstrate what they have learned and to choose how to present their evidence of learning. Rather than providing one opportunity for students to submit evidence by giving a multiple-choice test or assigning a project, this teacher provides acceptable choices for the students in the classroom and allows them to decide which option is the most suitable for them.

At the secondary level, a seventh-grade teacher assigns a response to literature writing prompt. Rather than provide questions, the teacher encourages the students to choose which questions they would like to write about.

Because these teachers provided voice and choice, they increased student engagement and empowered them to become self-directed learners. Students were allowed to explore their passions and feel honored for their judgment. Teachers must always have the mindset that they are not teaching a classroom, but rather the individuals in the room.

Self-Care

> It's not selfish to love yourself, take care of yourself, and to make your happiness a priority. It's necessary.
> —Mandy Hale

Self-care is anything that individuals intentionally do to take care of their mental, emotional, and physical health. Self-care is not a selfish act. It is about recognizing and responding to what you need to be an overall emotionally and physically healthy individual before caring for others. The old saying of "before you assist others, always put your oxygen mask on first" rings true for everyone, especially educators.

Ordinary tasks such as staying hydrated and getting bathroom breaks can be almost impossible, let alone managing the cognitive and emotional overload that comes with supporting and guiding all the students in the room as well as dealing with tasks assigned by the school site and the district. It is no secret that teachers are often overtasked and under-resourced, and to prioritize self-care can seem almost unattainable. But teaching can be emotional labor, and filling one's own emotional and physical tanks is incredibly important and beneficial, both for educators and their students.

When educators utilize self-care practices to maintain physical and emotional strength, they are setting an example for their students. Teachers who strategically use metacognition, bringing to light some of their personal dilemmas, help to normalize and encourage the use of coping strategies for students.

The focus on educator self-care should not land entirely on the teacher's shoulders. Teachers cannot be expected to share with students a resource that they may lack themselves. The trauma that students endure in their personal lives can take a tremendous toll on the educators responsible for teaching them. Consequently, teachers need dedicated space to talk about those experiences and to be able to more intentionally keep their own mental and emotional health stable.

Schools must institutionalize the precepts of self-care into school culture through the professional development embedded into the school year. Effective schools also take the initiative to foster self-care and healing during the school day.

Constructive self-care embraces a mindset that makes mental and physical health a priority and can look very different from person to person. While there are many resources that offer self-care suggestions, the key is to experiment and find what best brings physical and emotional wellness. Here are some resources to help you begin:

- The Teacher Self-Care Conference: http://teacherselfcare.org/
- *Teach and Take Time for You* by Cassandra Washington (2016)
- Self-care resources from Mindful Teachers: http://www.mindfulteachers.org/p/self-care-resources.html

- Workshops by Dr. Tina Boogren: https://www.nomoreboringmeetings.com/portfolio_page/dr-tina-boogren/

Revisiting What We Know

Let's revisit and address Jill's questions. What was causing this disconnect? Why did the students and their parents believe her motives to be insidious? What was Jill missing?

Jill, like many new teachers, was doing what she was trained to do. She took what she learned in her credential program, in instructional methods or classroom management strategy courses, and applied them to her daily routine. What Jill wasn't trained to do was handle the complexities of her students' diverse stories. Jill would contact parents about their child's misconduct and explain to the families what that student did wrong or how that student treated Jill.

Her rigid, one-size-fits-all behavior strategy was causing a disconnect with her students and families because she was addressing the outcomes, rather than focusing on the solutions. Perhaps the student who persistently used foul language in class needed more than the "pulling of a behavior stick" or "moving his clip" up and down a behavior chart. Jill cannot assume she knows the students' motives. When in the service of children, educators must first seek to understand. A student may need someone to genuinely sacrifice his or her time and energy, and build trust and respect, to see what would work best to address the use of bad language in the classroom.

Jill was mistaking kindness for care. This type of care was what was missing from her repertoire. She cared about each one of her students. But, in the infancy of her career, Jill was driven by teacher-centered philosophies. Her entire platform was based solely on what *she* was going to bring to the classroom. It took many children, families, supportive teachers, and educational researchers to restructure Jill's center. It wasn't until she flipped her mindset and provided genuine, authentic care, through equitable practices, that she saw a shift in her effectiveness.

Theodore Roosevelt stated that *Nobody cares how much you know until they know how much you care.* This is a profound statement that educators need to adopt as a crucial tenet of their vocation. Children and families require an amalgam of care and relationships. Whether it's a student in an affluent private school setting or a child in an impoverished, underserved public school, students deserve personalized care. Every child has a story.

READER TAKEAWAYS

- Caring for students includes building relationships so that students feel love and a sense of belonging.
- One of the best ways to build a relationship is to provide voice and choice.
- The most influential factor in positive student achievement is teachers attitudes or beliefs about the potential of their students.
- Caring for students equally is important, but caring for students equitably is crucial.
- Teachers are unable to authentically care for students until they attend to self-care.

REFERENCES

Hattie, J. (2016). *Visible learning for literacy*. Corwin.
Payne, R. (2003). *A framework for understanding poverty* (3rd rev. ed.). Aha Process, Inc.
Shalaby, C. (2020). Classroom management as a curriculum of care. *Educational Leadership, 78*(3), 40–45.
Sprenger, M. (2020). *Social emotional learning and the brain*. ASCD.
Washington, C. (2016). *Teach and take time for you*. Castel Publications.

TWO
Grief in the Classroom

Stephanie Heitkemper

> Grief is not a disorder, a disease or a sign of weakness. It is an emotional, physical and spiritual necessity, the price you pay for love. The only cure for grief is to grieve.
>
> —Earl Grollman

EXPECTED LEARNING OUTCOMES

- Readers will learn four steps for addressing death with an individual student.
- Readers will be able to comprehend death's impact on children per their developmental level.
- Readers will be able to identify ways to help students feel less alone in their grief through bibliotherapy and resource websites.

One in 14 children in the United States will experience the death of a parent or sibling before age 18 (Judi's House/JAG Institute, 2020). This roughly translates to two children per classroom, one child per baseball team, and three kids on every high school football team. Grief looks different at every developmental stage of life. In a younger child, grief is often displayed in magical thinking about the deceased and their return, behavior regression, central sensitization, guilt over "causing" a death, and helplessness. In adolescent children, grief is shown through increased trouble and concern with school or their own health, depression, and anger (DeSpelder & Strickland, 2020, p. 382).

It is inevitable that grief will one day enter the classroom. This chapter is designed to help educators compassionately and appropriately respond to each student's grief, based on the child's developmental level.

WHAT I KNOW

How to Address Death and Grief

When talking about a recent death with students, think of these four steps. This will help enhance connection with the student, keep a clear focus, and assist in balancing personal emotions to begin supporting a student's grief journey.

1. Gather information about the person who died. It is important to name the correct person, and that person's relationship to the student. If unsure, a simple way to phrase the question is, "I heard your family recently experienced a death, and I am here to support your grief journey. I don't want to be disrespectful; can you remind me of their name again?"
2. It is inevitable that adults want to help and protect students. Be careful with the words chosen. Avoid well-intended cliches such as "They are in a better place," "They are no longer in pain," "They lived a long life," or "I know how you feel."
3. Avoid euphemisms such as "went to sleep," "passed away," "loss," and "pushing up daisies." It is important that children (and adults) get comfortable with the truth to process the experience and integrate it into the reality of their lives.
4. Make time to hear about the deceased, and keep a note card with important information. This later can provide insight on potentially new or stronger grief reactions by the student. Using this card can help you increase connection with the student, too. For example: "You're wearing a Broncos jersey. I remember you telling me about the game you went to with your brother. He was a big fan!"

Things to include on the notecard:

- Student's name
- Name of deceased

- Age and date of birth of the person who died
- Date of death, including day of the week and approximate time
- Something the person who died really enjoyed
- Three words to describe the deceased

Holiday Tip: The information gathered on the notecard can also be revisited as educators navigate holiday celebrations in the classroom. Always ask the student, one on one and in private, about whether they wish to participate in such activities, and consider creating a back-up plan. Experience has taught educators that children still want to be included in making cards for deceased members of their family, or for those who have filled the role of that person. Students are the experts in their stories; trust their judgment.

Children's Development

The primary models for children's development include those by Erik Erikson and Jean Piaget. Erikson focused on the stages of psychosocial development, where personality and mastery is developed across eight stages beginning from infancy to adulthood (table 2.1). Piaget focused instead on the cognitive transformations across childhood (table 2.2).

A third, lesser-known model is Duey Freeman's developmental tasks model, as adapted by Heather Gunther, which provides insight to the alignment of emotional and chronological age. Recognizing development is crucial because when children experience death at a young age, they grieve over and over as they explore each developmental level.

Table 2.1. Erik Erikson: Stages of Psychosocial Development

Stage	Age	Title
1 (Infancy)	Infant–18 months	Trust vs. mistrust
2 (Early Childhood)	18 months–3 years	Autonomy vs. shame
3 (Preschool)	3–5 years	Initiative vs. guilt
4 (School Age)	5–13 years	Industry vs. inferiority
5 (Adolescence)	13–21 years	Identity vs. confusion
6 (Young Adulthood)	21–29 years	Intimacy vs. isolation
7 (Middle Adulthood)	40–65 years	Generativity vs. stagnation
8 (Mature Adulthood)	65+ years	Integrity vs. despair

Table 2.2. Jean Piaget Model of Development

Age	Developmental Period	Characteristics
Birth–2 years	Sensorimotor	Focuses on sense and motor, and understanding objects exist
2–7 years	Preoperational	Develops symbolic thinking
7–12 years	Concrete Operational	Applies logic to understanding of concrete ideas
12+ years	Formal Operational	Reasons logically regarding abstract ideas

Children's Development Regarding Death Comprehension

Children's ability to comprehend death can best be broken into four areas described by Speece and Brent: universality, irreversibility, nonfunctionality, and causality.

- Universality, as it applies to death, means that all living things must die; death can occur at any moment.
- Irreversibility refers to the understanding that once the body has died, it cannot be made alive again.
- Nonfunctionality refers to the understanding that after a living thing or person dies, all typical life-defining capabilities end, such as eating, hearing, talking, thinking, and moving.
- Causality is more abstract, combining internal and external factors that contributed to the death.

Typically speaking, older children understand universality before younger children. As younger children grow in their understanding of death, it is typical to struggle with comprehending irreversibility and nonfunctionality. On average, children fully comprehend these ideas between ages seven and nine (see table 2.4).

Reactions to Grief Based on Age

Reactions from preschool-age children (2–4 years) include:

- Crying
- Regression
- Increased separation anxiety

Table 2.3. Developmental Tasks: Duey Freeman and Heather Gunther

Age	Developmental Period	Characteristics
Conception–birth	Do I exist?	Often no language or eye contact
Birth–18 months	Is the world okay?	Behavior is unpredictable
18 months–36 months	Am I okay?	Child projects insecurities on adult caregiver
3–6 years	How much can I do?	Emphasis is on quantity vs. quality
7–11 years	How well can I do it?	Emphasis shifts to quality vs. quantity
11+ years	Who am I?	Combines all stages to make up self-identity

- Repetitive questions
- Direct explanation of the death to others

Reactions from elementary school–age children (5–10 years) include:

- Fear of abandonment or separation
- Increased physical complaints: headaches, stomachaches, and body aches
- Quick emotional reaction
- Change in energy, memory, appetite, and concentration
- Yearning to be with the deceased

Reactions from middle school–age children (11–13 years) may include:

- Wide range of varying emotions: guilt, anger, sadness, fear, joy, and confusion
- Change in social support needs
- Hidden separation anxiety that is denied to peers
- Thoughts of self-harm and suicidal ideations

Reactions from high school–age children (14–18 years) may include:

- Avoidance of grief
- Increased screen time
- Trouble concentrating and focusing in several areas of life
- Change in perceived family role
- Increased reckless or risk-taking behaviors (unprotected sex, experimental drug use, skipping school, or driving fast)

Table 2.4. Children's Grief Comprehension

Age	Developmental Understanding of Grief
3–5 years	Death is less than alive.
5–9 years	Death is final and can be avoided.
9+ years	Death is the result of a biological phenomenon. Death is personal, inevitable, and universal.

- Thoughts of self-harm or suicidal ideations

WHAT YOU NEED TO KNOW

Details to Consider When Exploring Reactions to Grief

Case Example: *It was the summer before second grade. On a warm summer day, it was typical for dad to take the dog on a run. They were best friends, and running was their special time. As the children played outside waiting for dad and the beloved pup to return, they saw a lot of commotion across the street. Neighborhood parents ushered the children inside. Together, the siblings sat close and compared notes on what they had seen. They really hoped the neighbor was okay. Unfortunately, the commotion wasn't around the neighbor; it was around their young father, who experienced a heart attack on his daily run. Everything changed instantly. Not only did the children experience the death of their father—they lost all sense of their consistent schedule.*

Who knew the special hug and handshake before school? Who knew the morning routine better than Dad? Dad remembered the details on the school calendar. Dad knew your favorite hot lunch choices without needing a reminder. Dad knew math, and how to make you have bellyache laughs before bed.

The common reactions to grief can be interchangeable across age ranges. In addition to varied reactions, educators must keep in mind each student's individuality. If the teacher is unsure whether one of the considerations listed below pertains to the student, it is okay to warmly ask the student. When it comes time to support grief, it is better to not assume and to not be sarcastic, as this can feel hurtful or offensive to the student.

Below is a list of considerations educators should keep in mind when exploring student's individual grief reactions:

- Student's personality and preferences

- Student's past experience of death
- Student's relationship with current caregiver
- Student's relationship with the deceased
- The nature of the death:
    - Anticipated vs. sudden
    - Age of the person who died
    - Any stigma around the death
- Secondary losses experienced by the student:
    - Job change, school change, moving, dating
    - Loss of self: identity, confidence, personality, and health
    - Loss of security: emotional, physical, fiscal, and lifestyle
- Student's gender and culture identity:
    - Community, customs, and beliefs
    - Acceptance around death and loss
    - Funeral and burial/cremation rituals
- Student's family dynamics:
    - Roles and responsibilities
    - Rituals and routines
    - Expectations and values
    - Beliefs and superstitions

Connecting Emotion and Logic with Grief

It is essential that educators meet grieving students with active empathy. This is easiest and most effectively accomplished by engaging the right side of the brain first. The right side is responsible for emotional intelligence and the processing of nonverbal cues. The right side of the brain makes sense of relationships and context. Upon activating the right side of the brain, educators can then add in the left side of the brain. This is the side of the brain where logic is interpreted, and students learn to make sense of the words and data, helping them to create boundaries. An easy way to remember this is first feelings, then logic. Some examples include:

- "Sam, you look scared. You don't want to be away from your mom today."

- "Katie, your tears make me think you are feeling sad, and focusing on the math test seems impossible."
- "This looks frustrating; it is hard to focus on Tuesdays at 1:00 p.m. Can we take a break?"

What to Do When Students Return to School Following a Death

Case Example: *A small group of middle schoolers met for a grief group. Each participant, newly bereaved within the last school year, was paired with a one-on-one adult mentor. One boy named Johnny spoke about how since his dad had died in a sudden accident, he hated school. This had become a significant point of conflict between Johnny and his mom.*

For the facilitator, it was important to stay curious. "What is the worst part of school since your dad died?" the facilitator asked. Johnny hung his head down, dropping all eye contact and said, "Every time I go to math class Sarah asks if we have enough food, or if her family can bring dinner . . . I know . . . I know . . . I know Sarah is trying to be nice, but then all I can think about is how much I miss my dad. Then I miss what the teacher is saying, and then I get confused. I am already behind in math since my dad died. My mom, she won't understand how upsetting Sarah's kind gesture is to me."

Johnny's story highlights understanding what is important to the student when he or she returns to school. Students need some control over their story. Unfortunately for Johnny, the town was small, and news traveled quickly of his dad's death. Even when school administration and staff are aware of details regarding the death, checking in with the student is valuable.

If at all possible, make contact with the student before they return to school. This can allow time to talk to the student about the return plan, designate a point person of the student's choice, put in place accommodations that may be needed, and explore how the student is beginning to cope with the death.

Do not assume that the person who died was a loved one. Allow the student the opportunity to inform involved, caring adults about the person who died. When speaking about the person who died, keep it simple. When connecting with the student, avoid saying the overused phrase "I'm sorry for your loss." Lead honestly with your body in acknowledgement of the death and, most importantly, listen to the student. Here are four important questions to ask the student:

1. What do you want your peers to know about the death?
2. If you need to take a break from class, where would you like to go? (It is best to create a pass that allows the student to exit the class at any time. Grief does not follow rules.)
3. Who on staff are you most comfortable speaking with?
4. What, if any, concerns/worries do you have about returning to school?

As the student prepares to return to school, talking through and writing down a plan can be valuable not only for the educator, but for the family of the student. Grief often leaves students and caregivers in a foglike state of anhedonia.

Time off from school varies by student. Some students need to take time away from school to begin their mourning process. For others, the routine of school feels safe and they will not take any days off. It is also usual for each student in a family to approach school and details differently. A common reaction is not wanting their peers to know about the death. There is no right or wrong way to approach school attendance or the amount of information a student wants peers to know.

Supporting Disease and Chronic Illness as It Applies to the School Routine

Case Example: *It is 1:30 p.m. on a sunny spring Tuesday, which meant students could eat outside. Eating outside is a perk of being an eighth grader, and Riley looked forward to the independence she had begun to earn not only at school, but at home with her parents. Today, however, felt different. By 1:45 p.m., Riley had a terrible stomachache and the teacher sounded exactly like the teacher from Charlie Brown. Minutes felt like hours, and Riley could not make sense of anything the teacher was teaching. You see, Riley's parents were with her younger sister. Today was the day they would learn the course of treatment for her sister's cancer. It was the second time the cancer had come back, and Riley felt helpless. To earn more responsibility, she choose to attend school, but in math class this was now her biggest regret.*

For students like Riley, the hope is the next round of cancer treatment provides a cure for her sister. As students navigate life-threatening disease, chronic illness, and even potential anticipatory grief as a family member approaches end of life, it is important to create a warm space where these sensitive topics can be approached in the same way as when a student experiences a death in the family.

Academic Considerations

Year after year, grieving students encounter so many kind, caring teachers who go the extra mile for them—educators who empathize, slow down, connect, and empower them and their needs. Sometimes it is reported as "the right thing to do"; others teachers have shared, "it's the only thing to do." Some even say, "I wish someone had done this for me." Whatever the motivation in helping the student adjust to this life-altering change, do not forget it. Even after routines return to normal, sports resume, and students become familiar with navigating life without the family member, academic considerations are still necessary.

Students often struggle with the way to convey the catch-22 feeling regarding school: how sometimes during intense feelings of grief they struggle to focus, hear instructions, complete assignments on time, and recall the information for the test, while at other times they want to feel "normal" and to not be treated any differently than their peers. This poses a fine balance.

Case Example: *Kate's mom had been on-and-off sick with cancer for as long as she could remember. Most years her teachers supported Kate as her mom endured treatments. This year was new; Kate was now in middle school and instead of one teacher, she had seven. Kate desperately wanted to tell the teachers about how her mom was dying. Her mom was frail, and each day Kate was scared her mom would die while she was at school. Kate couldn't muster up the courage to explain this experience to each teacher. Kate assumed it was a lot of pressure to expect her dad to communicate her mom's changes in health to the school.*

Kate's first four teachers were flexible and approachable. However, Kate struggled to connect with her sixth-period teacher. Kate's dad reached out on her behalf and was redirected to have Kate reach out directly to the teacher. Kate did not perceive this as helpful, and life at home got more hectic. Kate's grades began to slip after her mom died. She was not failing, but her work was not her typical performance. Her principal reported that she did not qualify for special academic support, but her brother in eighth grade did because he had a noticeable change. Kate's dad was heartbroken, baffled, and reported feeling like a failure that he couldn't get Kate the same support that her brother received.

Grief can lead students to attempt to keep their anxiety and discomfort a secret from teachers. Each state has different requirements for how students qualify for academic considerations, such as an individual education plan (IEP) or 504 plans. Grief is not predictable, and does not manifest in consistent behavior or triggers. Utilizing a written plan can help all teachers, administrators, and support staff in a school support the grieving student in a consistent and clear manner. A written plan can help set up students for future success in later grades. Below is a list of potential academic considerations that may benefit students. Incorporating these in a written plan can empower students to acknowledge their emotions using healthy coping skills, as well as maintain a balance between feeling grief and feeling normal like their peers.

- Designate a safe person at the school
- Implement a printed pass system to allow the student to take a break; these are sometimes called "cool down" or "pressure passes"
- Help the child navigate assemblies and/or large-group activities
- Help prepare students for changes in the schedule: routines, substitute teachers, field trips, and drills
- Preferential seating
- Extended time for testing
- Modification of test format and delivery
- Modifications in classroom and homework assignments
- Assistance with note-taking
- Modification of teaching
- Providing clear and simple directions for homework and class assignments
- Appointing "row captains" or "homework buddies"
- Adjusting class schedules
- Helping with organization (Sample Accommodations for Anxious Kids, n.d.)

Supporting Stigmatized Losses

When a death is associated with a stigma, students may experience periods of more intense and isolated emotions. Stigmatized losses include death by suicide, homicide, and overdose. One way to offer nonjudgmental support is to choose words very carefully to prevent adding shame, guilt, or stigma. Words like "committed," "dirty" versus "clean," or other negative ways to describe the cause of death should be avoided.

Research shows that it is valuable for children and teens to know the cause of death. This information should come from a parent or guardian first. Asking the parent or guardian before a student returns to school what details they are aware of is one way to prevent accidentally sharing information of which the student is unaware. Once a student knows the cause of death, it is important to address any stigma. Always remember that the cause of death does not define the person who died. Take time to hear students' emotions and memories regarding the death of their family member.

WHAT YOU CAN DO

Children's Grief Resources and Children's Grief Awareness Day

There are many organizations across that United States and internationally that support grieving children. Organizations such as Comfort Zone Camp, Camp Erin, and Experience Camp provide children with a camp experience in addition to connecting them with other grieving children to reduce isolation, learn coping skills, and share their stories. Peer-based support groups in school, and through bereavement centers and/or local hospices, can also create an environment where children can connect with others who have also experienced the death of a family member.

Children's Grief Awareness Day (www.childrensgrief awarenessday.org) began in 2008 to help generate more support for grieving children and is observed every year on the third Thursday in November. The goal of Children's Grief Awareness Day is to provide an opportunity to raise awareness for the needs of grieving children.

To create a space for grieving students in your school, invite them to participate if they choose. Acknowledging Grief Awareness Day can also help other students acknowledge their experience of grief. Some ways to show your school's support include:

- Wearing blue
- Creating a memory wall
- Using the Children's Grief Awareness logo, "Hope the Butterfly," to spread messages of hope
- Asking students their ideas and opinions

Case Example: *A few weeks ago, Maria received a group text message that her friend Elizabeth's dog had died. Another friend, Bridget, had instructed the girls to support Elizabeth as she navigated her emotions regarding her dog's death. Behind the scenes Maria felt sad. No one asked about her dad, who had* died just five months ago. Maria's counselor reminded her that sometime adults struggle with what to say to kids who have experienced the death of a parent or sibling, and that sometimes people are too scared of making the bereaved sad, so they avoid talking about the person who died.

The counselor reminded Maria that anytime she wanted to talk about her dad, or share a memory, she should. It was a way of having continued bonds with her dad. Maria's counselor shared about National Children's Grief Awareness Day. As the six-month death anniversary approached, Maria knew she was ready to educate her friends about grief. She even told Ms. Annie, her favorite school counselor, that she was going to wear blue to raise awareness. On the Children's Grief Awareness Day website, Maria found that the symbol was a blue butterfly.

On the third Thursday in November, Maria proudly wore her Camp Erin shirt, blue accessories, and asked her teacher if she could tell her classmates about why it was a special day. Ms. Annie printed and laminated blue butterflies for Maria to pass out to her class. Later that night, Maria sent her counselor a text message: "Hi, today I wore blue to show appreciation and support for Children's Grief Awareness Day. Ms. Annie printed and laminated blue butterflies to pass out to our class. I had a lot of fun and wasn't stressed at all. It felt so good to be the person to teach my classmates about grief. I can't wait to include more people next year."

Book Resources on Grief

There are many stories to help children relate to and understand grief. Some books are easier to connect with than other books. Some children need a direct message, whereas others can follow the narrative and relate to the main characters.

Titles appropriate for preschoolers:

- *The Goodbye Book* by Todd Parr
- *Maybe Tomorrow* by Charlotte Agell

Titles appropriate for elementary students:

- *The Invisible String* by Patrice Karst
- *Bug in a Vacuum* by Melanie Watt
- *When Dinosaurs Die: A Guide to Understanding Death* by Laurie Krasny Brown and Marc Brown
- *My Big Dumb Invisible Dragon* by Angie Lucas

Title supporting death by suicide:

- *Luna's Red Hat* by Emmi Smid

Titles appropriate for adolescents:

- *You Are Not Alone* by Lynne B. Hughes
- *Modern Loss: Candid Conversations about Grief* by Gabrielle Birkner and Rebecca Soffer

General Grief Support Resources

Supporting grieving students is not a job for one teacher, administrator, or school counselor. It truly takes a village to support each student's emotional needs. The National Alliance for Grieving Children is dedicated to providing national support for grieving children. The NAGC website (www.childrengrieve.org) has a directory to find support for students and their families by state.

In addition to the directory, NAGC offers many different types of resources and educational opportunities to support adults caring for children. The Dougy Center, located in Portland, Oregon is the National Grief Center for Children and families. For over 30 years, the center has trained other programs nationally and internationally. To view the comprehensive list of organizations utilizing the peer support approach, visit their website (www.dougy.org).

Self-Care Tips for Teachers

- Be kind to yourself. Responding to grief in your classroom may be new; this may feel similar to a personal story or may cause regretful feelings around approaching a student in a different manner. Recognizing and responding appropriately to emotions can only happen if educators treat themselves with the same kindness, attention, and optimism they use to support students.
- Don't forget self-care. It is important to remember the acronym DEER (Drink, Eat, Exercise, and Rest). Taking care of the body and brain allows educators to be the best version of themselves, which is important to students!
- You don't have to navigate supporting students alone. It is a great idea to collaborate with your school staff, administration, and district colleagues.

READER TAKEAWAYS

The hope is that this chapter serves as a touchpoint to help educators calmly and full-heartedly respond to a student's loss.

- Utilize the tables in the chapter to serve as reminders of developmental behavior and grief reactions.
- Educators do not need to navigate a student's grief and loss alone.
- Creating a clear and concise support plan with administration and support staff can ensure that a student begins to think of school as a safe place as they navigate grief.
- It is key to treat each response to a death as if it is the first time grief has entered your classroom. This fresh approach gives educators the ability to genuinely connect.

REFERENCES

Corr, C. A., Corr, D. M., & Doka, K. J. (2019). *Death & dying, life & living* (8th ed.). Boston, MA: Cengage.

DeSpelder, L. A., & Strickland, A. L. (2020). *The last dance: Encountering death and dying* (11th ed.). McGraw-Hill Education.

Judi's House/JAG Institute. (2020). Childhood Bereavement Estimation Model (CBEM). https://www.judishouse.org/cbem

Sample accommodations for anxious kids. (n.d.). Retrieved December 7, 2020, from Worry Wise Kids. http://www.worrywisekids.org/node/40

THREE

Recognizing and Responding to Commercially Sexually Exploited Children

Debbie Johnson and Katherine Grayson

> I am only one, but still I am one. I cannot do everything, but still I can do something; and because I cannot do everything, I will not refuse to do something that I can do.
> —Edward Everett Hale

EXPECTED LEARNING OUTCOMES

- Readers will be able to identify the common red-flag behaviors and high-risk factors of commercially sexually exploited children (CSEC).
- Readers will gain an understanding of the grooming process that sex traffickers use to exploit their victims' vulnerabilities and gain psychological control.
- Readers will develop intervention strategies for responding to suspected CSEC victims and explore prevention education strategies for the classroom.

Chapter 3

WHAT WE KNOW

What Is Sex Trafficking?

Sex trafficking is a form of human trafficking, defined as " the recruitment, harboring, transportation, provision, obtaining, patronizing, or soliciting of a person for the purpose of a commercial sex act, in which the commercial sex act is induced by force, fraud, or coercion, or in which the person induced to perform such act has not attained 18 years of age" (U.S. Department of State, 2000, p. 7). According to this definition, all commercial sex acts by persons under the age of 18 are considered sex trafficking. There is no such thing as a child prostitute; children by law cannot consent to commercial sex acts. Therefore students under the age of 18 who perform a commercial sex act are not making a poor life choice; they are the victims of a crime.

A commercial sex act is "any sex act on account of which anything of value is given to or received by any person" (U.S. Department of State, 2000, p. 6). The item of value does not have to be money. Youth who perform sex acts in exchange for food, drugs, or a place to sleep are being trafficked.

It is difficult to estimate the extent and prevalence of the commercial sex trade in the United States, in part because the crime is generally underreported and also because identifying and measuring victims and perpetrators can prove challenging (Developmental Services Group, 2014). Even when estimates are calculated and published, they often cite numerous qualifiers and caveats (Institute of Medicine and National Research Council, 2013).

While the entire scope of the issue is difficult to quantify, data does exist for identified victims and high-risk groups. In their *2019 Data Report*, the Polaris Project reported that 14,597 victims of sex trafficking had called the National Human Trafficking Hotline. This is a 20% increase over the number of calls in 2018. Of those for whom an age was recorded, 80% were minors. This data most likely represents only a small portion of the actual trafficking occurring in the United States (Polaris Project, 2019). On average, children first fall victim to commercial sexual exploitation between the ages of 12 and 16 (Greenbaum et al., 2015). In 2018, just over half of the criminal human trafficking cases active in the United States were sex trafficking cases involving only children (Currier & Feehs, 2019).

According to the Office on Trafficking in Persons, sex trafficking is:

> a public health issue that impacts individuals, families, and communities. Traffickers disproportionately target at-risk populations including individuals who have experienced or been exposed to other forms of violence (child abuse and maltreatment, interpersonal violence and sexual assault, community and gang violence) and individuals disconnected from stable support networks (runaway and homeless youth, unaccompanied minors, persons displaced during natural disasters). (2017, p. 1)

The U.S. Department of Justice estimates that 200,000 American children are at high risk of becoming sex trafficking victims (2004). While there are higher risk groups, "no child is immune to becoming a victim of child sex trafficking, regardless of the child's race, age, socioeconomic status, or location, and every child involved in this form of commercial sexual exploitation is a victim" (U.S. Department of Justice, 2020, p 1).

WHAT YOU NEED TO KNOW

Those who work with youth should not rely on victims to self-disclose. Traffickers use sophisticated grooming tactics on their victims, including threats, emotional manipulation, and violence. Because of this, victims are often unable to recognize their victimization, are frightened of retaliation or consequences from their trafficker, and are unlikely to come forward on their own (National Center for Missing & Exploited Children [NCMEC], 2020).

The following lists of red flags and high-risk factors can help educators identify students who may be at risk for trafficking or may have already become victims. The included vignettes are based on the experiences of actual victims of sex trafficking who were recruited during their high school years, and illustrate what it can look like when a student is being groomed and/or exploited. All names have been changed to protect confidentiality.

CSEC Red Flags

Certain behavioral and physical red flags are commonly present when a child is a victim of commercial sexual exploitation. The presence of one indicator alone does not confirm the existence of commercial sexual exploitation, but several indicators seen together does increase the likelihood that a student is being groomed or exploited (NCMEC, 2020).

- Signs of physical trauma or violence
- Inappropriate dress for weather conditions
- Hunger, malnourishment
- References to frequent travel or frequent hotel visits
- Evidence of hyperarousal: anger, panic, hyperactivity
- Evidence of hypoarousal: inability to bond, forgetfulness, flat affect/low emotional response
- Presence of controlling or abusive "boyfriend" or older male/female who is not a guardian
- Lack of control over personal schedule
- Looks to another before answering questions or lets others speak for him or her
- Has items or an appearance that is not expected for his or her current financial situation
- Carries multiple cell phones or electronic devices
- Preoccupied with "getting money," has large amounts of cash or pre-paid cards
- Has a name or symbol tattooed, burned, or branded onto his or her body (may attempt to conceal)
- Uses trafficking language such as "Daddy," "the game," and/or "the life" (NCMEC, 2020; Stanislaus County Office of Education [SCOE], n.d.; Smith et al., 2009)

In addition to these indicators, there are three red flags that, when even one is present, evidence clear concern that a child is being sexually exploited:

1. The student appears to be or indicates that she or he is being controlled or groomed by another person.
2. The student's internet, cell phone, or social media use involves (atypical for their age) social or sexual behavior.
3. The student spends time with people known to be involved in commercial sex. (San Mateo County Office of Education [SMCOE], n.d.)

Ana's Story

Ana entered freshman year as a top academic achiever; she was a 4.0 GPA student. Ana is athletic, disciplined, the eldest sibling. Early in her sophomore year she received a full-ride athletic scholarship for college. In fact, she will go on to skip junior year due to her academic capacity, all of this despite the fact that Ana's mom has had issues with drug addiction and spent most of Ana's teen years in rehab. Her father is an engaged single parent running a small business and taking care of his two daughters the best he can on his own.

During sophomore year, Ana met an older boy in his 20s whom she quickly began to call her "boyfriend." Ana's father noticed as she started to dress in a much more sexual manner and developed a rebellious attitude. She came home with a tattoo of this boy's name, which she tried to hide from her dad. She started to carry two cell phones and was often on the phone during school. In spite of her academic success, she began running with the students who cut classes and have gang affiliations. She sometimes put her head down and slept at her desk during class.

As things progress, her dad begins going to the school, begging for help. He struggles to convince anyone that something is wrong, because she didn't seem to be in any trouble. She has food and clothes; she looks clean. She is keeping up her grades. He feels he is being perceived as the one who has the issue—a helicopter dad, just trying to get attention and making his daughter the school's problem.

What is unknown to everyone is that when Ana's dad goes to bed at night, she is leaving the house and her "boyfriend" is selling her for sex multiple times per night. She gets home at 5:00 a.m. and is at her desk at school by 8:00 a.m.

Ana begins to recruit her younger sister to work for her trafficker. Before long, the younger sister goes to their father and tells him what's happening. At this point, her father is able to intervene and get them both into treatment.

CSEC High-Risk Factors

While all youth have vulnerabilities that can be targeted and exploited by a trafficker, the following risk factors place a child at higher risk due to increased vulnerability:

- History of unstable housing, multiple foster-care placements, or periods of homelessness/couch surfing
- Chronically running away from home
- Prior involvement with law enforcement/juvenile justice system

- Excessive truancy
- History of substance abuse or lives with someone with substance-abuse issues
- History of sexual abuse, sexual activity, or rape
- Has been kicked out of the home or stigmatized by the family for identifying as lesbian, gay, bisexual, transgender, or queer (LGBTQ).
- Learning disabilities or is an English language learner
- Lives in poverty or at a low socioeconomic level (NCMEC, 2020; SMCOE, n.d.)

Victoria's Story

Victoria is the oldest of four siblings, living with her parents in a mobile-home park. Victoria has recently arrived in the United States and is undocumented. Her parents don't speak English and are only intermittently employed. She herself is learning English as a second language. The family struggles with poverty and is receiving services through their county agency.

Victoria tests well below grade level at school. She is looking for a peer group but is having a hard time socially. She is poorly dressed, quiet, and shy. She sleeps on the floor in the hallway of the trailer and only leaves to walk to and from school.

After school one day she met an older man who has a car. He began to pick her up and take her out for fast food. She was happy to have someone who shows interest in her, feeds her, gets her out of the house. He seemed nice. They continued to spend time together and after a while, she considered herself to be his girlfriend. This gave her a sense of value and of hope for her future.

Soon her wardrobe began to change; she had nicer clothes and dressed more provocatively. She started getting her nails done. Her "boyfriend" picked her up at lunch and after school every day. By the end of her freshman year she began to miss classes. She got a dollar sign tattooed on her arm, next to a crown.

She went willingly the first time he asked her to have sex with his "friends." The requests increased to sometimes five or six times a night, sometimes during her lunch break from school. She did not want to lose this person who was providing so much for her, so she complied.

Her trafficker starts giving her methamphetamines to further her dependence on him and her compliance with his demands. She disappears her sophomore year and is found months later, abandoned, drugged, and half dressed in a park, having no idea how she got there. Law enforcement and Child Protective Services are called, and Victoria begins to receive treatment for her trauma and victimization.

Traffickers and the Grooming Process

Traffickers target vulnerabilities, and all people have vulnerabilities. Even children whose basic food and shelter needs are met and who come from a loving, stable home still have social, emotional, and identity needs. When a child is targeted, that child's particular vulnerabilities are carefully mapped and exploited by traffickers using sophisticated techniques. This means that every youth in the classroom, boy or girl, is potentially vulnerable to being a victim of this crime.

Traffickers can be male or female. It is common practice for a trafficker to eventually turn one of their victims into a recruiter. The recruiter/victim is then used to recruit more victims by befriending identifiably vulnerable youth of their own gender, and beginning the grooming process as a trusted friend.

Traffickers called "romeo" or "boyfriend" pimps use a grooming process to seduce their victims into a relationship and then, through increasingly violent and exploitative means, effectively brainwash their victim into having sex with strangers for money and turning that money over to the trafficker (Kennedy et al., 2007). The grooming process involves befriending a child, discovering his or her vulnerabilities, meeting the child's physical and/or emotional needs, and becoming a person that the child trusts and depends on. At some point, the trafficker may have sex with the child, claim to love them, and even call them a "girlfriend" or "boyfriend."

Traffickers then use intermittent reinforcement to condition the child to expect pain and abuse in addition to the positive attention, creating what is called a trauma bond. It is very difficult for children at this point to recognize that they are being controlled and used. They may believe they love the trafficker and have strong feelings of loyalty toward the trafficker even as they are threatened, manipulated, or forced into having sex for money. This grooming process is calculated and intentional. In fact, a book called *Pimpology: The 48 Laws of the Game* with chapter titles like "Prey on the Weak" and "When Pimpin' Begins, Friendship Ends" (Ivy, 2007) can be bought on popular online shopping apps.

Morgan's Story

Morgan entered her freshman year ready: dressed in all the best clothes with a designer backpack, hair highlighted, nails done, makeup and eyebrows perfect. Her mom dropped her off and picked her up in their Lexus every day. But Morgan had no friends and was being bullied by her junior high school peers on social media. Her dad, though present in the home, worked 80 hours a week. No one outside of Morgan's family knew that she was sexually abused as a child by a family member.

Morgan was isolated, lonely, and vulnerable. So when a junior boy took an interest in her, she was quickly drawn into his older circle of friends. Before long he began, to control who she could talk to and socialize with. He showed up at her classroom doors, and she was clearly afraid to upset him or keep him waiting. She started using her allowance and any gift cards she received to buy him name-brand clothing and sneakers. She believed they were in love. What she didn't know was that he was a second-generation pimp, with family in Las Vegas who were traffickers at an enterprise level. He was grooming her with the ultimate intention of taking her to Las Vegas and selling her for sex.

She and the boy continued to hang out for two years. During this time, he was seducing her, coercing her to do things she was uncomfortable with, videotaping her, and using ever-increasing violence to transform her. Once he had this kind of power over her, she was too scared to tell anyone what was happening. He began to dress her provocatively, hypersexualized. She started calling him "Daddy."

Neither of Morgan's parents liked this boy. They knew something was not right, but they didn't know what. Because he is a person of color, they were afraid to seem racist in their concerns about him.

Morgan disappeared her junior year. She was trafficked for two years on a circuit from Los Angeles to Las Vegas. It was only when her trafficker was arrested and put in jail (for trafficking a different girl) that she was able to break free and come home.

WHAT YOU CAN DO

Prepare to Respond to Individual Situations

With all of the challenges and expectations of being an educator, identifying possible sex trafficking victims in the classroom might seem like an overwhelming responsibility. But educators are in a unique position to observe their students regularly over a long period of time, during the years in which children are most vulnerable to traffickers. Armed with the right information, educators can be first responders in their students' lives. As first responders, educators *see* what is happening, *recognize* what is at stake, and can *dispatch* support services to those in need.

What to Do If a Student Comes Forward

- Make sure you and the victim are in a safe location
- Remain in a calm posture
- Assure the child that he or she was right to speak up and is not to blame
- Do not make promises about what will happen to the student or the trafficker
- Let the student tell the story; do not interview the child
- REPORT. For example, California law requires reporting as soon as possible, and a written report within 36 hours (SCOE, n.d.)

What to Do If You Suspect Human Trafficking

As mandated reporters, educators are legally required to report any suspected child abuse to child protective services and/or local law enforcement. This includes suspected sexual exploitation.

- Contact local law enforcement
- Make a Child Protective Services (CPS) report
- Inform appropriate school site administrators
- Monitor student and continue to report any new red flags or concerns (SCOE, n.d.)

Establish Campus Protocols

On a campus-wide level, staff and administrators should be trained to recognize and respond to commercial sexual exploitation of students. Protocols should be put in place to guide educators on how to handle suspected or confirmed trafficking cases. If your campus does not have protocols in place, advocate for them. Sample human trafficking educator protocols can be found on the San Mateo County Office of Education's "Preventing Human Trafficking" web page (SMCOE, n.d.).

Provide Prevention Education

Knowledge is power. Educators have the ability to advocate for their students to learn skills in various areas that make grooming and recruitment more difficult:

- Bring education specific to sex trafficking prevention into the classroom.
- Advocate for students to receive education on safe dating skills and relationship red flags.
- Advocate for students be educated about online safety so they can recognize how exploitation works on the internet and can protect themselves from traffickers and pornographers.

In addition to advocating for students to be educated in these three specific areas, educators can consider how overall cultural pressures and trends are affecting students and attempt to counteract these influences in the classroom. By teaching critical thinking, making room for reflection on cultural trends, and providing healthier messages, educators can directly empower students to avoid victimization.

Critical Thinking about Culture

A number of factors underpin the culture of sex trafficking. Two discussed below are sex as content and the targeting of males. Areas for further exploration include the glorification of pimp culture (especially in the music and film industries), gender expectations and biases, and the objectification of women and girls (Greenbaum, 2014).

Sex as Content

In addition to the ever-increasing sexualization of teens and tweens in all forms of media, the growth of the internet and social media is driving of the idea of sex as "content" even further into the cultural narrative. Sites like www.onlyfans.com are influencing a generation of kids to believe that taking pictures of their bodies is normal and they can get paid for it. On onlyfans.com, all you have to do is pose in your panties from the seeming safety of your own room, and people send you money and compliments. This is creating a generation of youth who will be more easily led into the grooming process, as they are preconditioned to think of their body and their sexuality as a commodity.

Boys: Targeted Three Ways

Though both males and females are targeted as victims, and both males and females can be traffickers, sex buyers are overwhelmingly predominantly male. A survey titled *Who Buys Sex?* published by the group Demand Abolition surveyed 8,200 men across the country to study behavior among sex buyers. They found that high-frequency buyers (defined as purchasers of sex on a weekly or monthly basis) are more likely to have started at a young age, and with the help or encouragement of others in their social networks. In this study, 43% of high-frequency buyers' first experiences were arranged for them by a friend or family member. Sex buying is "a cultural phenomenon that can be passed down generationally and reinforced by social networks that accept sex buying as normal" (Demand Abolition, 2018, p. 10).

Demand Abolition also found that pornography use is one of the accelerating factors that can lead to normalized beliefs about sex buying and influence the decision to buy sex (2018). Pornography use has also been shown to directly correlate with buying sex (Farley et al., 2011). There is no denying that the internet has revolutionized the availability and ease of access to pornography for children and adolescents (Hornor, 2020). A study by Wright and Donnerstein (as cited in Collins et al., 2017) of 15- to 18-year-olds in the United States found that 54% of boys admitted to intentional viewing of pornography.

It is not just girls whose lives are at risk from the sex trafficking industry. Boys are being targeted as buyers. Critical thinking about cultural norms around pornography and sex buying is a vital tool to help boys avoid participating in the sex trafficking industry.

READER TAKEAWAYS

The issue of sex trafficking is complex, global, and well beyond the ability of any one person to entirely fix. Nevertheless, there are steps that educators can take to help prevent their students from falling victim to sex traffickers and to help those who may already be victims to get the support services they need.

- Educators who understand what sex trafficking looks like and can identify the red flags of trafficking victims are able to serve their students as first responders. Their role on the front line is to recog-

nize what is happening, report to authorities, and help connect their students with services.
- Every school campus should have protocols in place for responding to suspected or confirmed trafficking victims among the student body. Educators can advocate for the adoption of campus protocols.
- Sex trafficking is a pervasive cultural and social issue that has developed in one-degree steps. Ending it will take place in one-degree steps as well. Some of those steps can take place in the classroom through prevention education and teaching critical thinking about cultural influences.

REFERENCES

Collins, R. L., Strasburger, V. C., Brown, J. D., Donnerstein, E., Lenhart, A., & Ward, L. M. (2017). Sexual media and childhood well-being and health. *Pediatrics, 140* (supp. 2), S162–S166. https://doi.org/10.1542/peds.2016-1758X

Currier, A., & Feehs, K. (2019). *2018 Federal human trafficking report*. Human Trafficking Institute. https://www.traffickinginstitute.org/federal-human-trafficking-report-2018/

Demand Abolition. (2018, November). *Who buys sex? Understanding and disrupting illicit market demand*. https://www.demandabolition.org/wp-content/uploads/2019/07/Demand-Buyer-Report-July-2019.pdf

Developmental Services Group. (2014). *Commercial sexual exploitation of children/sex trafficking*. Office of Juvenile Justice and Delinquency Prevention. https://www.ojjdp.gov/mpg/litreviews/CSECSexTrafficking.pdf

Farley, M., Macleod, J., Anderson, L., & Golding, J. M. (2011). Attitudes and social characteristics of men who buy sex in Scotland. *Psychological Trauma: Theory, Research, Practice, and Policy, 3*(4), 369–383. https://doi.org/10.1037/a0022645

Greenbaum, J. (2014, July 15). *Child sex trafficking and commercial sexual exploitation*. National Council of Juvenile and Family Court Judges Conference, Chicago, IL.

Greenbaum, J., Crawford-Jakubiak, J. E., & Committee on Child Abuse and Neglect. (2015). Child sex trafficking and commercial sexual exploitation: health care needs of victims. *Pediatrics Journal, 135*(3), 566–574. https://doi.org/10.1542/peds.2014-4138

Hornor, G. (2020). Child and adolescent pornography exposure. *Journal of Pediatric Health Care, 34*(2), 191–199. https://doi.org/10.1016/J.PEDHC.2019.10.001

Institute of Medicine and National Research Council. (2013). *Confronting commercial sexual exploitation and sex trafficking of minors in the United States*. National Academies Press.

Ivy, Ken. (2007). *Pimpology: The 48 laws of the game*. Gallery Books.

Kennedy, M. A., Klein, C., Bristowe, J. T. K., Cooper, B. S., & Yuille, J. C. (2007). Routes of recruitment: Pimps' techniques and other circumstances that lead to street prostitution. *Journal of Aggression, Maltreatment & Trauma, 15*(2), 1–19. https://doi.org/10.1300/J146v15n02_01

National Center for Missing & Exploited Children (NCMEC). (2020). *Child sex trafficking identification resource*. https://www.missingkids.org/content/dam/missingkids/pdfs/CST%20Identification%20Resource.pdf

Office on Trafficking in Persons. (2017, November 21). *Fact sheet: Human trafficking*. Administration for Children & Families. https://www.acf.hhs.gov/sites/default/files/documents/otip/fact_sheet_human_trafficking_fy18.pdf

Polaris Project. (2019). *2019 Data report*. https://polarisproject.org/wp-content/uploads/2019/09/Polaris-2019-US-National-Human-Trafficking-Hotline-Data-Report.pdf

San Mateo County Office of Education (SMCOE). (n.d.). *CSEC and human trafficking protocols for educators*. Retrieved December 20, 2020, from https://www.smcoe.org/about/county-office-of-education/news/preventing-human-trafficking.html

Smith L., Vardaman, S., & Snow M. (2009). *The national report on domestic minor sex trafficking: America's prostituted children*. Shared Hope International. http://sharedhope.org/wp-content/uploads/2012/09/SHI_National_Report_on_DMST_2009.pdf

Stanislaus County Office of Education (SCOE). (n.d.). *Human trafficking support guide for school district staff and administrators*. Author.

U.S. Department of Justice. (2004). *Report to Congress from Attorney General John Ashcroft on U.S. government efforts to combat trafficking in persons in fiscal year 2003*. https://www.ncjrs.gov/ovc_archives/ncvrw/ 2005/pg5l.html

U.S. Department of Justice. (2020, May 28). *Child sex trafficking*. https://www.justice.gov/criminal-ceos/child-sex-trafficking

U.S. Department of State. (2000). *Victims of Trafficking and Violence Protection Act of 2000*. (Public Law 106-386). https://www.govinfo.gov/content/pkg/PLAW-106publ386/pdf/PLAW-106publ386.pdf

FOUR

Homelessness and the Classroom

Educators Responding with Care

Kourtney Kauffman and Samantha Van Horn

> Sometimes the bravest and the most important thing that you can do is just show up.
>
> —Brené Brown

EXPECTED LEARNING OUTCOMES

- Readers will be encouraged to personally reflect on and challenge their perspective about students who are experiencing housing instability.
- Readers will identify, acknowledge, and amplify strengths of students who have experienced homelessness.
- Readers will identify needs driving atypical behaviors that are often a struggle for students with homelessness, and shape nonpunitive responses to these struggles.
- Readers will be able to conceptualize practical and applicable responses to students with consideration given to holistic approaches.
- Readers will be encouraged to explore additional resources to better equip their classrooms and enrich their understanding.

Chapter 4

WHAT WE KNOW

"No one stepped in."

"I don't think they even really saw me. They just saw what was wrong with my life and what I did."

"I think people mostly cared about doing their jobs and getting their stuff done. Not so much about what was going on with me."

"They were focused on the bad stuff I did. They didn't think to ask why I was really doing it."

These reflections on childhoods spent in unstable and transient housing show students' feelings of being ignored, unimportant, or not truly seen for who they were, but merely for their circumstances. In one such conversation, a youth stated that, if she could get a message across to all other kids in the same circumstance, she would want them to know "that they are important." While this seems like a simple statement, with more reflection it becomes more profound. There are many situations that can create an experience of a student feeling unimportant; one of the most poignant is that of the student who is homeless.

Homelessness is one of the many issues that plague today's students and negatively impact learning outcomes. The COVID-19 pandemic and subsequent shutdown of in-person schooling in many parts of the United States exacerbated the problem. Issues of inclusion and equity have been in the forefront of conversations around teaching strategies, classroom management, and the role of educators in this modern cultural landscape.

However, among the many issues that create extreme hardship physically, cognitively, socially, and emotionally, are hidden—and often undetected—homeless students. While accepted as a likelihood in many classrooms, teachers and school administrators are often left without the knowledge or skills to identify and support students who are experiencing instability in their housing situations.

Students managing homelessness in their lives can downplay, minimize, or deny their situation, often from fear, stigmatization, or avoidance of system involvement. However, these students often garner attention through disruptive, withdrawn, or difficult behaviors. Oftentimes, this creates a dynamic of frustration, irritation, or power struggles before the need behind the behavior can be identified and supportive resources can be found. Essentially, this means that teachers can often feel frustrated and impatient before even learning the needs that are driving behaviors and finding ways to connect students to necessary resources.

While an important part of the solution, educators and school personnel only represent part of the needed resources for families experiencing homelessness. A holistic approach to assessing needs of students, particularly those with housing instability, must be prioritized in order to fully support these vulnerable students and to promote the best outcomes, both academic and otherwise. Educators are often front-line responders who can find themselves overwhelmed or stressed by the volume of needs and struggles of their students, and by the lack of resources and coordinated efforts to support students identified as homeless.

Comprehensive understanding of the impact of homelessness is an essential first step toward a holistic approach to care for students and their families facing these kinds of challenges. To address one facet of the struggle without a balanced and open-minded perspective on the many concerns or needs that may be present can sometimes cause more harm than benefit.

This perspective is essential, even in beginning to examine the definition of the term "homeless." While some families can find shelter at relatives' homes or in transitional housing, some may be forced to live in hotels or vehicles. In extreme situations, students may go home in the afternoon to tents or makeshift shelters in hidden corners of their communities. While typical responses trend toward finding permanent housing solutions first, teachers can often find themselves overwhelmed by attempts to solve those kinds of intense and massive needs.

Addressing the immediate physical housing needs are important; however, that can require a larger, holistic and systemic response rather than the actions of an individual teacher. In some cases, teachers who jump to first respond to these larger needs rather than do the seemingly "smaller," more accessible responsive actions often find themselves overwhelmed and experience burnout.

Educators have a great influence, particularly when focusing their contributions to the needs of their vulnerable students in clear, actionable ways in the regular days and routine interactions they have with their students. If housing instability is a reality for a student, that student will search for stability in daily life; this can mean that classroom routines and rituals become the stabilizing force for vulnerable students.

Holistic and trauma-sensitive care for students facing homelessness is varied and is complicated by multiple factors: developmental and age-specific needs and behavioral presentations, academic background and foundation, the nature of the needs, regular nutrition, safe sleeping arrangements, presence of abuse or neglect and system involvement, among others. However, educators can represent a huge win in addressing these challenges through their ability to provide students with consistent routines, presence, and safety.

While these kinds of practical strategies may seem inadequate when compared to the daunting reality these students face, they are the essential foundation on which health and safety is built into the internal world of a student. For students with unpredictable and uncertain home situations, predictability—in any form—is safety. Teachers struggling to find the appropriate route to support their vulnerable students can find comfort in this simple truth and its practical application in their daily instruction.

WHAT YOU NEED TO KNOW

Homelessness is a multifaceted and complex problem. In a University of California, Los Angeles (UCLA) study, Bishop et al. (2020) report that in the last decade, student homelessness in California has increased by 48%; additionally, 27% of all people experiencing homelessness and 53% of all unsheltered individuals in the United States live in California.

Due to this upward trend, student and youth homelessness has become a problem at the forefront of educators' minds. However, it becomes important to further define what "homelessness" means in practical settings. The federal McKinney–Vento Act (1987) provides a legal definition of homelessness, which includes the following:

- Living temporarily in a relative's home
- Staying in a hotel
- Staying in a shelter or transitional housing
- Sleeping outside in a park or other area
- Living in a RV or vehicle
- Moving from dwelling to dwelling on a regular basis (i.e., family members from shelter to hotel to shelter)

Essentially, homelessness can sometimes be summarized at its basic level as an unstable living situation. This instability in a central part of a student's life can bring devastating consequences and results in a foundation for learning that is shaky and uncertain.

Impact of Homelessness

Understanding the impact of homelessness or instability on students in a holistic way is challenging. Multiple factors can result in varying student outcomes, including but certainly not limited to:

- Individual differences within person and personality
- Age at onset of housing instability
- Length of time homelessness is experienced
- Family history of trauma
- Food accessibility and nutrition history
- Access to medical care
- Inherent academic abilities
- Race and cultural factors
- Community factors
- Access to resources
- Immigration status

Because of the complexity of the impact of homelessness on students, it is vital to begin each interaction with your students with humility and curiosity, particularly when learning how homelessness affects a particular student. Humility ensures educators' intentionality in understanding their own bias and internalized stigma, and provides a framework for understanding those around them. Curiosity teaches educators to develop hypotheses about their students and student behavior, lightly and with discovery rather than "fixing" as the goal. This approach can help educators create a school community that is inclusive, reduces stigma, and provides empathetic support and resourcing for vulnerable students.

In many cases, it is helpful to consider the impact of experiences on students from a bottom-up approach, which means initially understanding the way a physical brain and body is impacted by housing instability, then moving to understanding its effect on socio-emotional development, and then classroom impact. As one nonprofit worker serving homeless individuals would say to volunteers, "Sometimes people can't hear what you're teaching or preaching at them over the grumbling of their stomachs."

In the same way, systematically addressing the needs of students who experience homelessness in a holistic way is often best approached first through physical impact, then beyond to the socioemotional, cognitive, and academic needs. In his 1943 paper, "A Theory of Human Motivation," Abraham Maslow first proposed Maslow's Hierarchy of Needs, a theory formally introduced in his 1954 book, *Motivation and Personality* (Maslow, 1987). His theory suggested that a person's development throughout life occurs in stages that require, to a degree, that specific needs be met prior to moving to subsequent stages. Most often seen as a pyramid, the needs are listed from basic (physiological) at the base and advanced (self-actualization) at the top of the pyramid. Although movement through each stage is not always linear, Maslow argued that a person must have met the most basic needs of the previous stage prior to having the motivation or ability to move to a new or different stage.

Respectively, the first two stages are physiological needs and safety needs. Once those needs are satisfied to a reasonable degree, a person moves to satisfy needs of love/belonging, esteem and, lastly, self-actualization. Physiological needs are defined as food, water, warmth, and rest.

For a student who is homeless, the first two stages alone pose quite a challenge. These students may have significant difficulty in satisfying the necessary threshold for progressing beyond physiological needs to the next "tier," safety needs. Safety needs are stipulated simply as security and safety. While a student affected by homelessness could progress past either of these to achieve higher levels of motivation, presumably it would be a difficult and long process, requiring significant and strong social connections, community connections, and self-awareness.

As physiological and safety needs form the foundation to motivate a child's climb toward self-actualization, it is important to consider what kinds of physiological needs are not addressed for students experiencing homelessness.

Physiological Impact

Among the dynamics of homelessness that impact the physiology of a student's growing brain and body, quality sleep becomes a commonly identified issue, but the impact of poor or restricted sleep time is rarely understood at a deep level. Getting an adequate amount of sleep has an incredible impact on overall functioning, making it perhaps one of the most essential parts of early human development, stress management, and overall quality of brain health—all necessary for student's learning. By understanding sleep on a deeper level, it becomes more apparent how important the quantity and quality of rest is for learning. Studies by the National Institute of Neurological Disorders and Stroke (NINDS) report that those who experience sleep disturbances experience a deterioration in the functioning of their nervous systems. Lack of sleep not only leaves a person feeling drowsy, but can "lead to impaired memory and physical performance and reduced ability to carry out math calculations. If sleep deprivation continues, hallucinations and mood swings may develop" (NINDS, 2007). Furthermore, "Activity in parts of the brain that control emotions, decision making processes, and social interactions is drastically reduced during sleep, suggesting that this type of sleep may help people maintain optimal emotional and social functioning while they are awake" (NINDS, 2007).

Essentially, while a student sleeps, the brain is working in two ways: it is synthesizing information that the child has received during the day, and it is allowing for crucial parts of the brain to rest and to be regenerated simultaneously. If sleep is interrupted or shortened, the brain does not have an adequate amount of time to go through the various stages of sleep needed for completion of these tasks for optimal functioning. This clearly demonstrates the struggle that low sleep quality presents to students in classrooms where emotional regulation, challenge, learning, critical thinking, and growth are a necessary part of their daily school lives.

For many reasons, those who are homeless experience a significant disturbance in their sleep duration and environment, often leading to sleep deprivation. The brain needs the rest and regeneration of protein-to-protein interactions that happen during sleep to develop along a normal physical, academic, and socio-emotional curve.

In a meta-analysis conducted by Pilcher and Allen (1994), they contend that a person's mood is more affected by sleep deprivation than a person's cognitive and motor abilities. Consequently, it is likely that students who are homeless are not primed for learning, retaining information, or significant mood regulation, putting them at a disadvantage when compared to rested peers.

It can be difficult for educators to determine their role in supporting healthy sleep practices for students, often because they sometimes jump to solutions (i.e., "I can't do anything about where they sleep at night"). However, it is helpful to consider instead the assessment of student needs. A student falling asleep in class, while sometimes a general irritant for an educator, can be a major indicator of coming or current academic struggle, among other things.

While the temptation is often to regulate errant sleeping behavior at an inappropriate time, educators would do well to consider first the needs that underlie the behavior, by asking themselves why the student is not well-rested and exploring their internalized reactions and beliefs about what made that student so tired during the day. This pause in reaction to reflect on needs works to slow educators' reactionary responses that can further destabilize the students' trust in the academic world.

Beyond sleep quality, the physical impact of homelessness seems such a straightforward part of the issue that it is often overlooked or oversimplified. While naturally moving to thoughts of personal hygiene or the lack of both personal and academic supplies, educators often move next to the idea that students experiencing homelessness may also need resources in the form of food and nutrition. While this is an important question, it is a faulty assumption to move to the belief that students in this situation are simply hungry and that food, any available food, solves the problem of hunger.

Like sleep, looking simply at surface concerns and meeting those needs, such as giving a snack to a hungry student, can often lead educators to feel a faulty sense of relief that the problem is solved, while in actuality, the growing brain and body of a student feels the impact of hunger in much more complex ways. Regular nutrition plays an integral role in brain and body development, and hunger signals are signs of biological danger, as humans require food to survive. Therefore, a lack of nutritive sustenance in a consistent way can have far-reaching consequences beyond hunger pangs. Issues caused by long-standing inconsistent food resources such as problems with memory (essential to learning), inefficient self-regulation mechanisms, intrusive anxious thoughts, and disruptive health issues can cause all manner of challenges for students working to maintain focus and concentration in a classroom during a long school day.

Beyond that, a brain compensating for food instability may look to behaviors such as stealing or food hoarding to satisfy the gnawing, underlying or unconscious survival anxiety, as well as the hunger. These compensatory behaviors can then serve to frustrate and alienate educators who are willing to help, but miss the student's underlying motivation and focus solely on the problematic behaviors.

Understanding how sleep and food instability can impact the outcomes for students experiencing homelessness in a physical way starts a well-rounded process for educators to develop an empathetic, humble curiosity about their vulnerable students. To further understand other physical impacts on students affected by housing instability, it is also helpful to explore a recent focus of research to better understand the impact of the brain's trauma response, especially when activated chronically over time, on student health over the long term.

One of the foundational studies that has shaped how researchers see childhood experiences as having long-term consequences is the Adverse Childhood Experiences (ACE) Study. Through a longitudinal study beginning in 1998 with nearly 9,000 participants, Felitti et al. (2019) examined the relationship between adverse childhood experiences (ACEs) and long-term health issues, disability, and disease, among other impacts on a participant's overall health.

Remarkably, the researchers found profound long-term implications for participants who had two or more ACEs beyond typically assumed mental health concerns, including an increased risk for cancer, heart disease, and even early death. Practically, this gave the medical community increased urgency to understand and hopefully prevent the adverse experiences of children, in particular traumatic experiences, and can provide some practical assessment strategies for educators working on the front lines.

Primarily, ACE scores can assist teachers in refining their assessment of students to determine who may be at risk for long-term struggles or who are currently experiencing difficult and sometimes debilitating situations such as homelessness. Secondarily, the knowledge of how such situations can impact a child over the long term into late adulthood provides additional motivation beyond academic needs for vigilance on the part of the teacher, who may be the only adult in that particular student's life who has the ability, vision, and knowledge to intervene in a crucial moment.

Utilizing the suggested resources at the end of this chapter, ACEs can be detected and additional resources, support, and care can be focused on the appropriate direction. While not exhaustive, these resources provide a helpful starting point for educators wishing to understand the experiences of their students and the long-term impact of those experiences on academic understanding, memory, attention, physical struggles, and many other concerns that tend to cause students to struggle in the classroom.

The Pediatric ACEs and Related Life Events Screener (PEARLS) is one such assessment developed by Koita et al. (2018) and includes homelessness as an additional life event that can bring similar levels of long-term impacts on children as other adverse childhood experiences. The PEARLS assessment identifies housing instability as a potentially traumatic event for a child, which can create brain pathways and physical impacts that can affect someone over the long term.

With several reporting methods, as well as English and Spanish versions, the PEARLS assessment is often utilized by medical and mental health professionals to identify and provide resources to vulnerable populations. For students impacted by homelessness, an increased risk of exposure to other potential traumas can be expected, including separation from parents, mental illness concerns, or possibly—although not inherent—neglect.

Impact of Trauma on the Brain

For educators, understanding how experiences of their students can impact long-term health outcomes can be an important motivator for the vigilance required for early detection and prevention of childhood trauma, and can be helpful in encouraging resilience.

The ACEs research makes a clear case for the impact of adverse experiences in childhood on long-term health outcomes. Experiences like homelessness can shape and impact the brain and learning. Furthermore, educators need to understand how trauma and adversity affect a young brain, as academic obstacles and impacts on learning are a primary focus.

When working to understand the brain in a state of trauma, it is important to note some basic but essential ideas. First, the function of the fear system in the brain is, at its basic level, to attain and maintain safety—to keep the "self" alive. Within that system, the brain works to assess whether something is a danger or is safe. However, one of the fundamental things to understand about that system is that the fear system (sympathetic nervous system, or SNS) is not concerned with how real a danger is; the SNS does not always efficiently distinguish between a real or perceived danger. It will have the same reaction whether or not the danger is real.

What this can mean for humans who are in a chronic state or feeling of danger (i.e., not knowing where they will sleep that night, or next week, or next month) is that the brain essentially gets stuck in hyperdrive and will begin to perceive that ambiguous situations, like learning something new or being called on in class to answer a question, is danger. People, and especially children, see predictability as safety. Therefore, unpredictability in a living situation creates a fairly constant state and perception of danger.

A second essential function of the brain's fear system is to establish a survival plan. This sounds like a thought-out, efficient process that the brain works through; however, in actuality this is a rapid assessment of the best way to escape the situation or get away from the danger as quickly as possible (i.e., the fight, flight, or freeze response). That rapid assessment is often based on quick perceptions and history. The brain will often sort through the most relatable experiences and history and apply the pattern learned to the current situation. This can result in repeat patterns to stress, which can seem erratic or destructive but make sense in this larger context. For example, if a student perceives that a lie has helped them escape a danger (i.e., helped them escape police questioning), they may continue using that strategy at other times (to avoid a consequence in a classroom setting). The pattern makes sense when underlying needs and trauma responses are taken into account, rather than taking the behavior at face value.

While this knowledge and theoretical understanding can feel tedious to educators eager to take action to improve supports for their students, understanding the complexities of student experiences and the short- and long-term outcomes bring necessary background and foundation; educators often find that the theoretical understanding builds patience when working with students struggling with problematic behaviors driven by underlying needs.

WHAT YOU CAN DO

Setting the Stage for a Sensitive Classroom

Given what has been explained about trauma and the brain, it is important that educators consider how they can help keep the brains of their students, especially those experiencing housing instability, in a place of learning as opposed to a place of survival. To further emphasize the impact this "survival brain" has on learning, we strongly suggested that educators watch a short video by Dr. Jacob Ham (see the suggested resources at the end of the chapter). The video illustrates how difficult it can be for students to learn while in a survival state, and the benefits for all when educators become more astute in identifying students' underlying needs, provide essential anxiety-reduction techniques, and maintain a robust self-care practice.

Paraphrased from the clinical treatment model in the book *Seeking Safety* (Najavits, 2003), all behavior represents a need. If an educator can adjust his or her perspective on a child and that child's challenging behavior to encompass this exploratory approach, it aids both the teacher and the student to create a more positive classroom environment. Difficult behaviors become overwhelming and are identified as a major challenge in the classroom, often due to the stress of managing a classroom of many personalities, behaviors, and learning styles.

While it is important for children to feel as though they have a certain amount of autonomy or ability to affect their environment, not every difficult interaction or challenging behavior is a struggle for power. It is often freeing for educators to realize that a student's behavior, at any given age, is trying to show a need that the child may not have the verbal ability to express. This can help focus attention to the heart of the issue and away from the distraction of the child's challenging presentation, and places the student and teacher on a level playing field to solve the problem together.

Assessing the needs of students as demonstrated by behavior can sometimes leave educators feeling lost. However, simple reflective questions asked before taking action can make a substantial difference in an educator's response. Ask reflective questions such as:

- Given what is known about this child, what might the behavior be communicating?

- What need might the student be trying to get met?
- Considering Maslow's hierarchy of needs, is there something in those fundamental levels that the child is struggling to somehow meet?
- Does the student need support, praise, to have fun, to know what is expected of him or her? Does the student need to learn a new skill?

There could be a variety of needs that underlie challenging behaviors. If the child cannot identify a need verbally, the educator can switch strategies from trying to have a face-to-face conversation (which can sometimes be intimidating to someone in an activated survival state) to taking a walk, offering a snack, or suggesting some deep breathing prior to asking them about their behavior or need. The educator simply reflecting on the idea that the child's behavior is just a representation of an unmet need can relieve tension in otherwise challenging interactions, and shift momentum from a power struggle to collaborative problem solving.

Adapting a Strengths-Based Perspective

Another way for teachers to support the learning of homeless students is through exploring their strengths and focusing on building resiliency. Traditional perspectives within the field of psychology often focus on identifying and treating adverse symptomology. However, over the past 70 years, the field of psychology has adapted its perspective to include important shifts that focus more on the positive aspects of life such as building meaning, identifying strengths, feelings of happiness and thriving, and resiliency.

The wisdom offered by positive psychology can help educators support students who have experienced homelessness to build personal values/assets within themselves and amplify their strengths. Any significant time spent with a child that has had to overcome hardships often reveals not only the challenges they face, but the incredible strengths and skills they have to offer their community.

While students may not have a diagnosis of posttraumatic stress disorder (PTSD), a helpful guide for framing observable strengths is the Posttraumatic Growth Inventory (Tedeschi & Calhoun, 1996). It identifies five aspects of a person's life that can become more significant or develop as a result of having a difficult experience: 1) relating to others, 2) new possibilities, 3) personal strength, 4) spiritual change, and 5) appreciation of life. Teachers can utilize this framework as a starting point for specifically identifying and amplifying strengths in children who have been through adversity.

Because children and teens who have experienced homelessness have been forced to adapt to a variety of circumstances, it is not surprising that many of them can be incredibly creative problem-solvers or see new possibilities where others perceive a lack of opportunity. These students often have had to become resourceful and find ways to get a need met when it seems impossible. While they may not even see this potential within themselves, educators may be able to amplify these strengths through specific and descriptive identification and praise of the student in real time.

In this vein, teachers wishing to support their vulnerable students become coaches, working to identify with specificity the strength and resilience that is embedded in their students. For some of these students, simply completing a homework assignment requires ingenuity and creativity; at perhaps no other time has this been a more accurate statement than during the 2020 COVID-19 pandemic.

Considering the struggles of distance learning, students experiencing housing instability lack the resources to access reliable technology and the internet, or may struggle to have a quiet place to work or even a cleared workspace on a consistent basis. Continuous consideration of the resources needed to complete classwork, whether through distance learning or in person, can be helpful for these students; however, more long-term impacts on students' positive sense of self may be found by encouraging the creative solutions they generate themselves.

An additional strength to note when considering students who experience housing instability is unique relationship skills. Loyalty to a relationship is often a high value among students who have had so much taken from them. While there has been some criticism over the years about Ruby Payne's *A Framework for Understanding Poverty* (Payne, 2005), she makes one assertion that appears to ring true in the lives of many homeless youth.

Essentially, because their possessions are few, Payne proposes that for students living in impoverished situations, important people often take the place of valued possessions. The staff, peers, administrators, or teachers identified by the student as safe or connective are sometimes treated as if they were the student's precious belongings. These relationships sometimes become territorial, and can cause conflict among their peers; nonetheless, the relationship skills required to build these connections and the loyalty that drives them seem to indicate the strength of "relating to others" as noted by the Posttraumatic Growth Inventory.

Additionally, considering all that has been presented here regarding students experiencing homelessness, it stands to reason that clinging tightly to relationships could be a matter of survival for these students. In many cases, because physical possessions are often inaccessible to them, these students may consciously or unconsciously spend time honing the skills that affect how they relate to other people. Often, they can win over the new student in class or do surprisingly well in an interview due to the social adaptability and charm they have developed through their life experiences.

The loyalty that can be inspired by this value can motivate students to feel fiercely protective of and guard that relationship. This high appraisal of personal relationships means that they will feel considerable love and care when these coveted relationships have been cultivated; it meets a survival need. However, it can also be a significant wounding if there is hurt or dissent that takes place in one of these relationships because it threatens meeting that need.

And like the value vulnerable students may put on relationships, some students from hard places also find profound appreciation and gratitude for items or experiences that others may see as trivial or minimal. They may not only appreciate the seemingly insignificant things that other students may overlook, but may also appreciate the way that staff, other students, or school personnel have taken part in their life or shown them recognition.

Whether they celebrate a C+ on a test or get excited over a pair of shoes that fit properly, some students adapt a perspective of appreciation for each positive moment, particularly if they feel they have previously gone without those experiences or if other positive events have been tainted by extreme stress or worry. Though it may not be every student, some may choose to cling tightly to experiences that bring hope and treasure the evidence of that along the way.

Another potential strength of students who have experienced homelessness as shown in the Posttraumatic Growth Inventory is personal strength or sense of purpose. These students have deep empathy for those going through hardship, born out of their own endurance of difficult situations. Sometimes these very experiences, although deeply painful, can be a driving force for creativity and allow for a deep sense of purpose. This often spurs a passion for creating a different life for themselves and for those that have experienced similar difficulties.

Educators have a unique opportunity in those formative times. Helping a student define and develop their passion can be a life-altering gift, particularly for children who have experienced extreme hardship such as homelessness. Educators play a crucial role in developing this strength by providing these children with different experiences, positive/specific praise, and clear, attainable goals in order to fight for a future that is different from their present. This truth gives life to the contention of Holocaust survivor and psychologist Viktor Frankl, who was fond of quoting Nietzsche "Those who have a *why* to live, can bear almost any *how*" (Frankl, 1962, p. 9).

If you, as a teacher, can observe any of these strengths in your students, call it out. Be specific in recognizing which resilient trait is present and clearly tie it to the behavior the student demonstrated. Many educators find an important shift in their mission from academic goals to viewing their role as responsible for exploring and excavating strengths within their students. Every student has something to offer; some realm in which they excel. While the strength may not be tied to their academic performance, it may be found in a multitude of important ways: how these students relate to their classmates, their quick wit, how they champion the underdog, or how they use creativity in their play. Educators should work to imagine with them how their strengths can turn into long-term success. Teachers have the unique privilege of being able to inspire and portray a world full of possibilities to their students and, as a result, they can develop hope and a path forward for students who have had trouble finding their way.

Tools for the Classroom

While changing lenses from academic performance to identifying and amplifying strengths is a powerful reframe for many, without a particular plan or practical application of theoretical knowledge, educators can be left feeling overwhelmed by determining which daily practices can support students with such struggle in their lives. The following suggestions can help to incorporate actionable strategies to an educator's toolbox.

Regularly Practice Self-Care

While it may seem surprising to start with a focus on educator's actions toward themselves, how people care for themselves determines how much time, energy, and effort they are able to give to others. Therefore educators, particularly those beginning their careers, should give careful consideration to practicing healthy self-care on a regular basis. While the term "self-care" is sometimes reduced to meaning pampering oneself, understanding true and healthy self-care can be impactful. As one workshop leader noted, "Self-care and self-comfort are different." Simply defined, self-care is making daily decisions that create a healthier life; self-comfort is the decisions and actions that feel comforting in the moment. While these ideas can overlap, simply beginning to evaluate daily activities in order to incorporate balance between self-care and self-comfort can be a powerful start to establishing healthy patterns in work-life balance for educators looking for longevity in their career without eventually succumbing to jaded perspectives.

Students from hard places can demonstrate their needs through extreme and frustrating behaviors, and teachers, whether new or seasoned, are well-advised to incorporate and develop healthy self-care decisions on a regular basis. For those most vulnerable students, an educator who is managing stress well is more present and mindful, and may act as a lifeline for vulnerable students.

Create a Trauma-Sensitive Classroom

Developing a trauma-sensitive approach to a classroom environment can be simple, yet effective. First, as discussed earlier in the chapter, predictability is safety for students who have experienced hard, unpredictable things in their lives. Therefore, establishing routines and rituals in the classroom and preparing students adequately for transitions or changes is an important first step. Second, consider using mindfulness techniques at the beginning of the class time, or as a part of the daily routine.

Recent attention and research have focused on incorporating mindfulness in the classroom, and mindfulness is often cited as helpful in soothing unregulated brains in both children and educators alike. Doing a few minutes of deep breathing, guided visualizations, or focused attention on something like a "singing bowl" can do wonders for calming squirming bodies or focusing frazzled minds. In some teachers' experiences, students begin requesting these techniques during stressful times in the classroom, such as preparing for a test.

Lastly, consider having items available that can support a student's regulation switch from survival brain, such as: a small piece of dark chocolate (preferably with lower sugar; the antioxidants are brain-supportive), a bottle of water, something with a strong but pleasant smell, a healthy snack, or a drink with light carbonation. If a student is truly in a survival state, these small tricks may help activate other parts of their brain and body, encouraging the brain to switch out of its stress response.

Have Travel-Sized Items Available

Having basics on hand such as toothbrushes, toothpaste, basic clothing (socks, shirt), travel-sized deodorant, or soaps can be tremendously helpful if a student shows up at school and needs these items. Instructing a student about good hygiene or allowing them to freshen up if they haven't had the opportunity will not only help that child feel more prepared for the day, but could support the student socially as well.

Ask questions of administration about availability of resources or how to support a cohesive staff approach to ensure that the items can be accessed in times of need. In some cases, school staff have created pathways for taking in donations of unused travel-sized goods from hotels and storing them in an easy-to-access place. While it is not the job of the school to provide these things, it can make a world of difference in a stressful moment.

Create a Habit of Identifying Student Strengths

Good intentions can often fall by the wayside when facing the stressors and dynamics of the classroom. Utilize the previous discussion on student strengths by regularly sitting down and naming the strengths of your students, particularly those with which it is most challenging to connect. Consider a written list or a visual representation of strengths in a place easily viewed, or leading regular discussions for students to identify strengths for themselves and each other, as well as to identify growth in themselves and others.

Get Curious

Remember, behavior represents need. Therefore, find ways to incorporate a curious outlook, particularly when working to regulate responses to challenging situations and behaviors. Asking questions such as "What is this behavior saying?" and "What new thing can be learned from this?" does wonders for gaining a degree of separation from emotional reactions, and helps educators to remain mindful in the midst of stress.

Practice the Skill of Empathy

Author Suzanna Stabile (2018) tells the story of an educator who created an immersive experience for the parents of her students, which would forever change their perspective of their child. The educator taught and assisted students with visual impairments that impacted their learning. She asked each parent to put on glasses that mimicked the specific visual impairment that their child suffered from, in front of their child, and asked the adult to perform simple tasks.

Through this, the parents were able to see how much adversity each child had to overcome just to participate in the classroom. Not only did the parents gain admiration for their children; the children received the praise they so desperately deserved.

Even deep parental love can sometimes miss the depth of understanding that empathetic reflection and exercises can demonstrate. Regularly find ways to move from sympathy toward empathy. Consider these helpful reflection questions:

- If I were to put on the life-lens of this child, what would I see?
- How would I feel?
- What might I need that I might not be getting?
- How can I connect with this child?

Self-Educate: Resources

Educators should consider the following resources to help them further their understanding and develop approaches that are sensitive to the complex issues of their students.

- Daniel Siegel's work has proved him to be an expert on the neuroscience of attachment. His 2012 book, *The Whole-Brain Child*, can

help teachers further their knowledge about mindfulness practices and how to implement these tools.
- Consider reading chapter 4 of *The Connected Child* (Purvis et al., 2007) to further your understanding of the fear response in children, spotting such responses, and disarming a child experiencing fear.
- As mentioned earlier, we highly encourage educators to watch the short video *Understanding Trauma: Learning Brain vs Survival Brain* on YouTube (Ham, 2017), which illustrates the differences between a learning brain and a brain in a survival state.
- Consider watching the YouTube playlist created by the Karyn Purvis Institute of Child Development (2018), specifically for educators. These provide a primer on why it is important to focus on connection, and some quick tools to use with primary students.
- Watch Dr. Nadine Burke make a compelling argument about the long- and short-term effects of childhood trauma. She also discusses her role in the development of the aforementioned ACEs. The questionnaire can be accessed by watching *How Childhood Trauma Affects Health across a Lifetime: Nadine Burke Harris* on YouTube (Burke, 2015).

READER TAKEAWAYS

- Educators play an important role in support, identification, and resource-connecting for students experiencing homelessness.
- Homelessness in students is a growing issue and impacts students in all areas: academic, social, emotional, and physical.
- Effective responses to student homelessness must include strategies to address multiple areas, including strengths-based approaches, trauma-sensitive classroom management, and accessible resources.
- Educators will be best suited to respond empathetically to students experiencing homelessness when they have been adequately prepared through self-education, reflection, self-care, and ongoing resource gathering.

REFERENCES

Bishop, J. P., Camargo Gonzalez, L., & Rivera, E. (2020). *State of crisis: Dismantling student homelessness in California*. Center for the Transformation of Schools, School of Education and Information Studies, University of California, Los Angeles.

Burke, N. (2015, February 17). *How childhood trauma affects health across a lifetime: Nadine Burke Harris*. [Video]. YouTube. https://www.youtube.com/watch?v=95ovIJ3dsNk

Felitti, V. J., Anda, R. F., Nordenberg, D., Williamson, D. F., Spitz, A. M., Edwards, V., Koss, M. P., & Marks, J. S. (2019). Relationship of childhood abuse and household dysfunction to many of the leading causes of death in adults: The adverse childhood experiences (ACE) study. *American Journal of Preventive Medicine, 56*(6), 774–786. https://doi.org/10.1016/j.amepre.2019.04.001

Frankl, V. E. (1962) *Man's search for meaning: An introduction to logotherapy*. Hodder and Stoughton.

Ham, J. (2017). *Understanding trauma: Learning brain vs survival brain*. [Video]. YouTube. https://www.youtube.com/watch?v=KoqaUANGvpA

Karyn Purvis Institute of Child Development. (2018, May 8). *TBRI in the classroom*. [Video Playlist]. YouTube. https://www.youtube.com/playlistlist=PL9WCXSvAXd6N_xZampTIofRri1K-9ar6a

Koita K., Long, D., Hessler, D., Benson, M., Daley, K., Bucci, M., et al. (2018). Development and implementation of a pediatric adverse childhood experiences (ACEs) and other determinants of health questionnaire in the pediatric medical home: A pilot study. *PLoS ONE, 13*(12). https://doi.org/10.1371/journal.pone.0208088

Maslow, A. H. (1987). *Motivation and Personality* (3rd ed.). Pearson Education. (Original work published 1954)

McKinney–Vento Homeless Assistance Act. (1987). Office of the Law Revision Counsel, U.S. Code. https://uscode.house.gov/view.xhtml?path=/prelim@title42/chapter119/subchapter6/partB&edition=prelim

National Institute of Neurological Disorders and Stroke (NINDS). (2007). Brain basics: Understanding sleep. National Institutes of Health/NIH Publication No. 06-3440-c. https://www.ninds.nih.gov/Disorders/Patient-Caregiver-Education/Understanding-Sleep

Najavits, L. M. (2003). *Seeking safety: A treatment manual for PTSD and substance abuse*. The Guilford Press.

Payne, R. K. (2005). *A framework for understanding poverty* (4th ed.). aha Process Inc.

Pilcher, J. J., & Huffcutt, A. I. (1994) Effects of sleep deprivation on performance: A meta-analysis. *Sleep, 19*(4), 318–326. https://doi.org/10.1093/sleep/19.4.318

Purvis, K. B., Cross, D. R., & Sunshine, W. L. (2007). Disarming the fear response with felt safety. Chapter 4 in *The connected child* (pp. 47–72). McGraw-Hill.

Siegel, D. J., & Bryson, T. P. (2012), *The whole-brain child: 12 revolutionary strategies to nurture your child's developing mind*. Bantam Books.

Stabile, S. (2018). *The path between us: An enneagram journey to healthy relationships*. IVP Books.

Tedeschi, R. G., & Calhoun, L. G. (1996). The Posttraumatic Growth Inventory: Measuring the positive legacy of trauma. *Journal of Traumatic Stress, 9*(3), 455–471.

FIVE

Children of the Incarcerated

Nita Brady

> Jesus said, "Let the little children come to Me, and do not forbid them, for of such is the kingdom of heaven."
> —Matthew 19:14

EXPECTED LEARNING OUTCOMES

- Readers will gain an understanding of how students are negatively impacted by their family members' incarceration in jail or prison.
- Readers will be provided statistical data, information, and personal stories of this impact on students.
- Readers will be given information and resources on how to approach students to provide tools, strategies, help, and support.

WHAT I KNOW

My journey into the world of children of the incarcerated has been a long one. This journey did not begin with these children, but with incarcerated youth at the local juvenile detention. Working full time at a large hospital at the time as a staff development educator, I didn't have much time for other involvements, especially volunteer work. But the pull to work with these incarcerated youth—some as young as 11 years old, up to age 17— was compelling and strong. Resistance was futile. This journey has lasted for 25 years, and has been eye-opening and heart-wrenching, to say the least.

During my weekly visits, getting to know the kids, their backgrounds, their place in the family, and whether or not they had family members who were also incarcerated, was fairly easy to ascertain. The vast majority had parents, siblings, aunts, uncles, and grandparents who were either currently incarcerated or had been incarcerated in the recent past.

So, when I later learned that, according to national studies, "70% of children with incarcerated family members become incarcerated themselves" (Vallas et al., 2015), it validated the experiences I noted within the local community. Twenty-five years of interactions with incarcerated youth not only proved that statistic to be true—but actually fell short of reality. It was much higher.

Since these incarcerated youths were always quite willing to share their personal issues, and were also very receptive to what was shared with them—as their emotional, spiritual, and practical needs were addressed—the question loomed large of whether any difference could have been made in their lives if they had received these coping skills and support at much younger ages. Would different choices have been made?

Another huge issue most of these children had was drug abuse in their families and in their own lives, which is what eventually led to their incarceration. The percentage of youth going down the drug addiction path, according to studies, is also the same as for children who eventually follow their family members into incarceration—about 70%. Of course, the consequences of drug use often go hand in hand with incarceration.

So, although the benefits of earlier intervention for these vulnerable children seemed essential, it was not realistic to get involved at that time. After retiring from full-time work at a large hospital system in June 2013, something happened that changed everything. Three women, independent of each other and with no foreknowledge, basically asked the same question: was there anything, any kind of program or outreach for young elementary and middle school children, who had incarcerated family members?

It was a legitimate question and concern, which was pondered and explored. Watching grandchildren suffer from the results of their fathers' addiction and perpetual incarceration cycle made it deeply personal. With retirement now a reality, the timing seemed right.

But how to go about this was a big question. Research would need to be done, a program needed to be developed, a team would need to be put into place, contacts would need to be made, school officials and parents/legal caregivers would need to be on board, children would need to be identified and signed up, and much planning would need to be done.

With the skills and knowledge from working over two decades as a hospital educator and 25 years working with incarcerated teens, we developed a program, trained and put into place a team, obtained the support of school officials, counselors, and community center leaders, and identified and signed up the children most at risk. "Beyond the Walls for Students" was off and running.

WHAT YOU NEED TO KNOW

To prepare for this huge undertaking, a lot of research was done. One of the many resources used was a book by Nell Bernstein titled *All Alone in the World: Children of the Incarcerated* (2005), which gave much insight into the lives of these children. It was truly heart-wrenching: how so many of these children carry a heavy burden of guilt, blaming themselves, carrying such shame, and deeply grieving the loss of an incarcerated parent, grandparent, or older sibling.

Some children have both parents incarcerated, and either have to move in with other family members or go into foster care. Many of these children are angry and have behavioral problems at home and at school. Many withdraw and become very depressed. Many have a hard time concentrating in school, due to the worry and fear regarding their incarcerated family members.

Often, this situation takes a huge financial toll, which causes resentment and frustrations for all in the family. Many children lie to cover up the truth to their friends; there is definitely a stigma. And sadly, many, due to their sadness, shame, guilt, and anger, go down the drug path, which eventually leads to their own incarceration.

According to research (Sparks, 2015), one in three children have externalizing issues: aggression, attention problems, and disruptive behavior. More than half have experienced the co-issue of substance abuse in addition to the incarceration issue. Three in five students experienced a change in family structure, due to divorce or separation as result of incarceration or drug abuse. More than one-third of these children witnessed domestic violence.

According to an additional study conducted at University of California, Irvine, "The most striking finding is that in some cases parental incarceration can be more detrimental to a child's well-being than divorce or the death of a parent" (UCI News, 2014). Parental incarceration and drug addiction significantly correlate to learning disabilities in children, including attention deficit disorder and attention deficit hyperactive disorder (ADD and ADHD), behavioral problems, and developmental delays. There are higher rates of asthma, obesity, depression, and anxiety as well.

Across the United States, there are currently 3 million children who have an incarcerated parent, and over 5 million have had a parent who was or is incarcerated. One in five children have family members who are incarcerated, and one in five have internalized issues of depression, anxiety, and withdrawal (Murphey & Cooper, 2015).

Armed with facts to better understand the issues these children of the incarcerated live with, and strategies to help these children break the cycle of drugs and incarceration, the program was developed. Both compassion and knowledge would be used to approach these students and provide them with coping skills and support.

The program would address these needs, and utilize powerful stories, visuals, role plays, tactile objects, positive coping skills, impactful speakers, a relaxed environment, healthy snacks, and the power of being in the presence of accepting others to whom they could relate: the power of the group dynamic. It became apparent that these strategies in this setting worked more beautifully than could ever have been imagined!

We gathered a team of people who committed to either helping facilitate a group or to lead one. Although it was not absolutely necessary to utilize people who had been touched by the prison system in some way, it was highly desirable. These people would have an insight and a passion that others outside this experience might lack. Some highly skilled, deeply caring, and passionate people with a shared vision joined the program to create a team. There has never been a single regret in this decision.

This important work began about seven years ago at a local community center and from there progressed to elementary and middle schools.

School counselors, teachers, principals, and family members have been very supportive and invaluable to the process.

The school counselors can identify which children are struggling due to drug use or incarceration issues in their families. Sometimes teachers refer these students to the school counselors. Sometimes parents or grandparents will contact the school to get help for their children in these situations. It is a collaboration, and requires trust and good communication. The school counselors are supplied with a letter describing the support group sessions and what they can offer the students, as well as a permission slip for parents and caregivers to fill out and return.

WHAT YOU CAN DO

Valuable resources have been utilized in these support groups, some specifically for elementary students and some targeted for the older children in middle school. A list of these resources and a website is provided at the end of this chapter for convenience. Each book includes a lesson plan that can be used by any teacher, school counselor, social worker, parent, youth worker, or clergy member who work with these vulnerable children—all at no charge.

The goal is to put valuable resources into the hands of teachers, school counselors, and others who desperately want to help these children with their issues. These resources have the potential to make a major difference for children who are struggling, particularly in the support-group setting, when possible.

To illustrate the effectiveness and the power of the support-group dynamic, a few stories must be told. One such story takes place at a middle school with some students who were particularly wounded. (All children's names have been changed to protect their identities).

It was a sunny spring day when 11 students at the middle school filed in for their first session of Beyond the Walls for Students, a series of eight one-hour classes in a support-group setting. A colorful banner with the group name and logo was prominently displayed at the front of the class. At each place around a large table there was a healthy snack along with a folder and name tag. The group was comprised of six boys and five girls.

Since this was the first session of the group, looks of curiosity and nervousness could be seen on their faces, which is very typical. They dropped their backpacks in the designated area, signed in, and then sat around the table at a place of their choosing. The students quietly exchanged looks with each other as they were warmly greeted by the two facilitators and the school counselor. Once everyone was settled in, introductions began. The purpose of the group was explained to the students, along with what they could expect, and the number of sessions.

The first session is entitled "What's Your Story?" and the head facilitator began to share her own personal story of her experiences of having close family members incarcerated and the impact on herself as well as young family members. The students listened quietly and respectfully, every eye on the facilitator. They were then encouraged to share their own stories.

It typically takes about three sessions for many of the students to feel comfortable enough to open up and share the impact of their family member's incarceration and to be able to trust the facilitators and other students in the group. Initially, they typically only share their name, age, and who in their family is or was incarcerated.

The students also have a short questionnaire to fill out, which provides more detail about their situation. Most students are willing to do this, though some are not yet comfortable speaking in front of the group about their family member's incarceration and how it has impacted them.

But this particular session proved to be quite different. A young boy, age 11, spoke up, gave his name and age, and then said, "My dad has been in prison since I was five years old, and I really miss him." Tears began to stream down his face, and he lowered his head. He was thanked by the facilitators for his willingness and courage to share what was on his heart.

This empowered the next boy, who was a couple of years older, to speak up and share that his mother was a drug addict who lived on the streets, and his father was in prison, so he lived with his grandparents. He shared that his grandfather, who was the only one he felt really loved him, died about a month earlier. As tears filled his eyes, he said he hoped to become a drug counselor someday to help families who might be in the same situation in which he found himself. Again, facilitators thanked him for sharing and for his courage. Something special was happening in this group; it was palpable.

This last confession further emboldened the third boy to speak up. After sharing his name and age, he stated through tears that his father, who had been involved in gangs and drugs, had been shot and killed "execution style"; that his mother drank all the time; and that he was in charge of getting his younger brother to school every day. He was only 12 years old. As tears spilled out, he added that he sometimes really felt alone. At this point, the young girl beside him turned to him and said, "Look around this table—you're not alone. We all have a story and we're here for each other." The boy smiled through his tears and thanked her. It was an incredible moment!

The school counselor and facilitator both clearly felt the power of what was happening in this group: the students were feeling it was a safe place to share their hearts and their concerns, discerned they were not alone, and found out that they would be well supported by each other and by these caring adults.

In the weeks that followed, the coping skills, support, and information shared with these students continued to empower and encourage them. By the end of the eight-week session, they were not the same students who walked in that first day, nervous, afraid, and upset. The counselor later confided that the classes really had a positive impact on each student.

Furthermore, the students were even opening up to the campus security man, sharing their concerns and their feelings, which had never happened before. These students definitely benefitted from the group, built relationships with the other students, learned they were not to blame, learned how they could manage strong emotions, learned new positive coping skills, and heard some dynamic speakers who had walked in their shoes at one time and are living proof that there is hope for a successful future—free of drugs and incarceration. All of these students seemed very grateful to have a group like this to share these very personal feelings and issues.

At an elementary school, something similar happened. A student in the program, Vanessa, said that she didn't know exactly when it all started with her mom. She didn't really notice it at first, but then her mother started acting strangely; she would stay in the bathroom all the time, and when she came out she wouldn't really talk to Vanessa or her little brother.

Then her mom would leave the house. Vanessa was left to fix dinner for her brother and herself, but there was never anything to eat. Her mom stopped coming home at night, and when she did, her mom and dad would just start fighting. There was always screaming and yelling. Vanessa was sure the whole neighborhood heard it. And sometimes her dad called her mother terrible names, and even hit her. Then one of them would leave the house.

During these terrible arguments, Vanessa's little brother would wake up and start crying. Vanessa would always go in and lay down with him in his bed, and sing to him to try to drown out their voices—but the screaming and arguing could still be heard. Eventually her dad left them, and her mom went into a drug rehabilitation facility. Now Vanessa and her little brother are living with their grandmother. Vanessa was beginning to wonder if her mom and dad really loved them. The other students listened attentively and quietly. The female facilitator squeezed her shoulder and thanked her for sharing what was in her heart.

Then another student in this group, Sarah, shared that that was how she felt about her dad, that he didn't really love her. His drug addiction took him first to jail and then to prison. When Vanessa asked her why she didn't think her father loved her, Sarah replied that he never wrote or called her. The other students asked if she wrote to him. Sarah answered that she did, but she never heard back from him. Tearfully, she said she found out that he does call and write to his "other family." At this point, Vanessa got out of her chair and went to where Sarah was sitting, put her arm around her, and softly said, "Well, we love you. And we're here for you. That's what this group is all about."

At another elementary school, an 11-year-old boy named Ryan spoke about his big brother whom he had always admired. Ryan talked about how this big brother began to change, how he became angry and mean all the time, and how worried his mother and he became when his brother stopped coming home.

When he did come home, he was meaner and more violent than ever. He would even hit their mother and make her cry. Ryan would try to help, but his brother was so much bigger than him. He really couldn't do anything. Then one day, the police came to their door; that was the day Ryan found out that his brother was dead—shot in the head. The students listened intently, some of them with tears in their eyes. Ryan shared that he heard the cop tell his mom that someone had shot his brother because of a drug deal that went bad.

Tears rolled down Ryan's cheeks as he shook his head. "If only my brother hadn't started taking those stupid drugs . . . " He put his head down on the table and all the students stared at him; it was something some of them secretly feared—their family members dying in some way because of drugs. One of the boys spoke up after a few minutes, and told Ryan that he was very brave to share what he did, and added softly, "We're here for you."

At another middle school, the lead facilitator was told by the school counselor that one of the girls in the group was so distraught over her father's incarceration that she had already tried to end her life. By the end of the eight-week session, this girl's mother told the school counselor what a huge difference the group had made for her daughter. The group itself and the information and strategies that were shared in the class had a very positive impact on her child. She said it made a world of difference for her; her attitude and outlook were greatly changed for the better.

These children of the incarcerated experience a large degree of stress. One of the sessions conducted in the support groups is called the "Three S's—Strategies for Stress and Sadness." It emphasizes positive rather than negative ways children can manage their stress, and multiple ways to help themselves feel better when they start experiencing the stress due to their family member's incarceration or drug use.

The students are asked to define stress, and the different types of stress are discussed: emotional, mental, and physical stress. Then the students are asked to share how they can tell they are really stressed, what they do, and how they feel.

Typical responses are that they feel tensed up inside or they feel like breaking things. Other times they just want to run away. Sometimes they cry a lot, mostly in secret. Sometimes they go into the bathroom or somewhere else on the school grounds where no one can see them cry. Sometimes they say they can't sleep, or once they go to sleep, they keep waking up and then they're tired at school the next day.

Sometimes they share that they don't want to eat or talk to anyone. Sometimes they just want to be by themselves. Some share that they eat too much. Some share that they get angry and they feel like they're going to explode and they just want to yell at people, especially younger siblings.

Once they have shared how they feel when they are stressed and what they do to handle it, they are then asked to think about some positive things that they could do to help themselves when they are feeling stressed. One of the students is chosen to be the group scribe, and lists some of the ideas on the whiteboard. They are encouraged to call out a positive strategy. Below are just some of the positive coping skills they typically call out:

- Listening to music
- Drawing, painting
- Talking to someone whom they trust about how they are feeling
- Playing sports
- Getting together with friends
- Praying and going to church
- Paying attention to what is going on inside of them
- Not allowing anyone to make them keep secrets but to share with an adult they trust (teacher, counselor, youth worker, family member, pastor)
- Reading good books
- Writing in a journal
- Taking deep breaths
- Punching a bag or pillow
- Crying to just get it out
- Yelling into a pillow
- Going for a walk
- Running
- Playing with their pets

In a session called "Whose Fault Is It?" the subject of misplaced guilt is discussed, and a humorous but impactful skit is performed by the facilitators to bring the point home. Many people do not realize just what a burden these children are carrying on their shoulders.

When asked if they ever felt like their family member's incarceration is their fault, most of the hands go up. If only they could have helped their dad, their mom, their sibling . . . if only they had done more . . . if only they hadn't caused their parents to be stressed, which caused them to do drugs, which led to their incarceration . . . if only they had done better in school . . . if only their behavior had been better . . . if only they hadn't called the cops on their dad who was beating their mother . . . if only they had warned their mom who was doing drugs in the other room, when the police came knocking . . . the list is endless, and the guilt is heavy.

All of this leads to a robust discussion of choices—and consequences. When individuals make a good choice, there is typically a good consequence; when individuals make a bad choice, there is typically a bad consequence. It is communicated in these sessions that people are only responsible for the choices they make, not the choices that others make. By the end of this session, these students are always set free from that guilt. They write this on their feedback forms and it is visible on their faces.

Sometimes special speakers are utilized, and have a great impact on these students. These are adults who have "walked in their shoes"—people who know what it's like to be a child that has a parent or close family member who is incarcerated, yet they were able to overcome the stigma and dysfunction, make positive choices, and become successful, productive, emotionally healthy individuals. It is not only an opportunity for these speakers to empathize with these children, but to infuse hope into these students as they share their powerful stories.

Children's lives can be changed with a concerted effort, one child at a time. This brings to mind "The Star Thrower" by Loren Eiseley (1978, p. 172):

One day a man was walking along the beach, when he noticed a boy hurriedly picking up and gently throwing things into the ocean.

Approaching the boy, he asked, "Young man, what are you doing?"

The boy replied, "Throwing starfish back into the ocean. The surf is up and the tide is going out. If I don't throw them back, they'll die."

The man laughed and said, "Don't you realize there are miles and miles of beach and hundreds of starfish? You can't make any real difference!"

After listening politely, the boy bent down, picked up another starfish, and threw it into the surf. Then smiling at the man, he said, "I made a difference for that one."

Caring adults can all make a difference in the lives of these children. It is imperative—not only for their sake, but for the sake of their families, and their communities. Like the message in "The Star Thrower," even the most caring adult may not be able to save them all, but certainly individuals have the power to make a positive impact on some, and quite literally, save their lives.

READER TAKEAWAYS

- There are positive actions that caring adults can utilize to help children of the incarcerated.

- Educators, working closely with families, are important in addressing the needs of these students.
- Compassion and patience are much needed. Ask the question: Why is this child acting out, or why are they disengaged? There are resources that can help (such as the books listed below).

Resources

These and other books with lesson plans (all free of charge) can be obtained at www.decisions.org.

The Little House Who Didn't Lose Hope (2nd edition), with lesson plan, by Nita Brady (2020). A present-day parable for any child who has ever felt marginalized, bullied, or abandoned; themes of choices/consequences, drug prevention, support, hope.

Zeeko, The Bunny Who Lost His Way, with lesson plan, by Nita Brady (2020). Strong themes of choices/consequences, drug prevention, support, hope.

The Dragonslayers Club, with lesson plan, by Nita Brady (2019). Powerful true stories of children in the support groups, told in a narrative form, and how they find help and hope.

REFERENCES

Bernstein, N. (2005). *All alone in the world: Children of the incarcerated*. New Press.

Eiseley, L. (1979). The star thrower. In *The star thrower* (169–185). Times Books.

Murphey, D., & Cooper, P. M. (2015, October). *Parents behind bars*. Child Trends. https://www.childtrends.org/wp-content/uploads/2015/10/2015-42ParentsBehind-Bars.pdf

Sparks, Sarah D., (2015, February). Parents' incarceration takes toll on children, studies say. *Education Week*.

UCI News. (2014, August 18). Parental incarceration linked to health, behavioral issues. University of California, Irvine. https://news.uci.edu/2014/08/18/parental-incarceration-linked-to-health-behavioral-issues-in-children/

Vallas, R., Boteach, M., West, R., & Odum, J. (2015, December). Removing barriers to opportunity for parents with criminal records and their children: A two generation approach. Center for American Progress. www.americanprogress.org/issues/poverty/reports/2015/12/10/126902/removing-barriers-to-opportunity-for-parents-with-criminal-records-and-their-children/

SIX
Becoming a Bodhi-Teacha

Actualizing Antiracist Practices

Amelia Herrera

Mrs. Thompson, with tears in her eyes, whispered back. She said, "Teddy, you have it all wrong. You were the one who taught me that I could make a difference. I didn't know how to teach until I met you."
—Elizabeth Silance Ballard

EXPECTED LEARNING OUTCOMES

- Readers will begin to develop a baseline understanding/working knowledge of what it is to be an antiracist and abolitionist teacher/educator.
- Readers will build capacity to actualize "equity talk" and put it into an "equity walk."
- Readers will begin actualizing the concepts of antiracist and abolitionist education in the classroom.
- Readers will understand the role of the "non-thinking" part of the brain and how it can play an adverse role in relating to students, if not checked.
- Readers will develop an understanding of the Buddhist concept of *bodhichitta* and what it means to educate students with this variation of love.

- Readers will gain ideas on how to re-evaluate and evolve teaching practices to align with culturally responsive pedagogies.

WHAT I KNOW

Have you ever been assigned five new students, from five different countries, speaking five different languages, in one week? For teachers of immigrant, refugee, and asylum-seeking students, this is a common occurrence. In fact, these students and the countries they represent are a direct reflection of the shifts taking place in the world. One could even say that classrooms like this are a history lesson in real time. It is a whirlwind to say the least. It is stressful. It is exciting. It is challenging. It is sometimes heartbreaking. It is humbling. Yet, it is oh-so-fascinating.

As fascinating as it is, there is an overwhelming amount to be learned about these students, including their life experiences, primary language(s), level of literacy in the home language, educational background, and their cultural and political ontology. Yet, what stands out as the most important aspect of this learning is a variation of *love* that can only be adopted when caring professionals begin to see past students' bodies and into their hearts. Teaching through this variation of love has proved more beneficial than any other piece of information learned about my students.

To be clear, the variety of *love* being referred to is not the variety of love that a teacher has for her students after a relationship is developed over time. It is the type of love that exists when a teacher *chooses* to love her students before she meets them or knows anything about them. It is a kind of love that is given simply *because*, without judgment or evaluation. It radiates out to students without expectation of love in return. It can be felt even when there can be no verbal exchange. This version of love allows a teacher to see students' hearts long before the teacher begins to learn their minds. This love holds space for any human, from anywhere, with any educational ability, who walks through a classroom door.

This form of *love* is what Buddhists call *bodhichitta*, a Sanskrit term referring to a mind that wants nothing more than to benefit and love all living beings (Rinpoche, 2019). *Bodhichitta* fosters the ability to love all students and allows us to be *fully awake* when we first meet them. What this means is that no matter who the student is, where he or she comes from, what languages the child speaks or doesn't speak, what clothing the child wears, and whether that child is smelly, or has boogers, or is combative and rude, the *bodhichitta* mind sees *nothing* distinct about a student at the first meeting, thus allowing the teacher to then see *everything* amazing about that student. Those teachers who can love their students like this are "Bodhi-teachas."

WHAT YOU NEED TO KNOW

Educators working with a globally diverse group of students year after year learn that not one cultural difference is too big for the *bodhichitta* style of love to defeat. Therefore, if love stands stronger when pitted against the constructs of cultural differences—the roots of racism, discrimination, and white supremacy itself—these, too, can be dismantled using the same weaponry. Unfortunately, educators know all too well that these institutions are deeply embedded in the structure of every American system and organization. Included on this list is the U.S. education system.

Those students most adversely affected by this system are black, brown, and historically marginalized groups. On top of the racial bias and discrimination impacting these students is the lack of access to curriculum that highlights their excellence, leads them on a path of self-awareness, and heightens their socio-political consciousness. Within the same system, yet in a different vein, students who are not black, brown, or marginalized are also being done a disservice.

Through curriculum, school policies, double standards, and educators themselves, these students are continuously shown that their lives matter more, that their history is the only one that matters, and that their race is the most superior. This miseducation has been proved to have little effect in reversing racism, discrimination, and white supremacy. Instead, it has done everything to perpetuate it. It's time for us to stop this destructive pattern.

Thus, to begin dismantling and rebuilding the education system, core understandings and pedagogies fundamental to this work must be learned and put into action. These understandings and pedagogies include being committed to abolitionist and antiracist teaching/education, ensuring that educational equity permeates every aspect of a classroom, and committing to using curriculum that helps students make sense of their own lives.

In addition, educators should also come to understand modern science research, particularly as it pertains to how our bodies react to others based on the "non-thinking" parts of the brain. This is important research to note because its findings reveal that subconsciously, teachers may be projecting their implicit biases and fears onto students. Underpinning it all, however, is the educator who strives to cultivate *bodhichitta*, a mind that seeks to benefit every sentient being without exception or exclusion because that person loves others as much as a mother loves her child (Rinpoche, 2019).

Dismantling Inequities by Building Understanding

So what is abolitionist teaching anyway?

In her book, *We Want to Do More than Survive,* author Bettina Love (2019) writes that abolitionist teaching is the act of thinking about "new ways to establish an educational system that works for everyone, especially those who are put at the edges of the classroom and society" (p. 88). Students put at the edges of our classrooms are most often black and brown students, newcomers, English learners, homeless students, foster youth, or students utilizing special education services.

Abolitionist teaching is the act of liberating those children from the margins of our classrooms and bringing them back to "center" by showing them that they matter and are loved. The work of an abolitionist teacher focuses on "working in solidarity with communities of color while drawing on the imagination, creativity, refusal, (re)membering, visionary thinking, healing, rebellious spirit, boldness, determination, and subversiveness of abolitionists to eradicate injustice in and outside of schools" (Love, 2019, p. 2). It empowers students through validating their histories, identities, and literacies (which includes how they use language) by creating curriculum responsive to each child's cultural and intellectual needs (Muhammad, 2020).

The historically responsive literacy framework (HRL), the brainchild of teacher-researcher Gholdy Muhammad (2020), is a perfect example of abolitionist curriculum. It focuses on the development of students' identities, skills, intellect, and criticality in such a way that they gain confidence in using learning "as a personal and sociopolitical tool to thrive in this world and to help them know themselves" (p. 68).

The HRL framework also seeks to dismantle and disrupt the limitations of traditional school curricula and its oversaturation of Eurocentric histories and ideologies by replacing it with curricula responsive to the social and cultural lives of the students in front of us. This framework is in direct alignment with the pursuits of an antiracist educator, or one who chooses to call out the ways that subject-matter curriculum perpetuates traditional ideologies, traditional educational systems, traditional curriculum, and long-standing American institutions that still function in the service of white supremacy (Lyiscott, 2019). An antiracist educator is one who pushes for equitable communities, schools, and classrooms and works to undo unjust systems, then "creates new ones built upon the collective vision and knowledge of dark folx" (p. 55).

The *action* involved in abolitionist teaching, antiracist curriculum, and culturally responsive and relevant pedagogy is the actualization of how Dr. Pedro Noguera proposes to achieve equity in our current educational system. In his latest Edutopia video on the state of race and equity in the U.S. school system, Noguera (2020) says that now that "we are seeing the inequities . . . what you have to do is change the conditions in school. . . . You don't have to change the kids or their culture."

In concert with the equity-in-action pedagogical styles and frameworks of scholars such as Love (2019), Lyiscott (2019), Ladson-Billings (1995, 2014), and Muhammad (2020), Noguera believes that to reduce inequities in the educational system, there will need to be "a massive reorganizing of the way we deliver instruction" (2020) and that "We'd need to move away from talking at kids to much more interactive, much more applied learning . . . we'd make schools that are developmentally focused on the needs of the children." (2020).

WHAT YOU CAN DO

The efforts of a caring adult cannot be underestimated. There are so many ways children and young adults can be supported by educators, counselors, and other influential adults in their sphere. The following list provides some ways to practically support children and youth.

- Think of "equity" as a *verb*-an *action*, not as a *noun*-an *idea*.
- Learn each of your students' histories, identities, and literacy and language practices (Muhammad, 2020).
    - Engage in general conversation with your students.
    - Seek out students' families and talk to them.

- Assign autobiography-like assignments.
- Assign "quick writes" that help students think about and discover new things about themselves. Have them share out so everyone, including you, can learn about them.
- Take a quick language survey to see what languages are represented in your classroom.

- Conduct an equity audit on the curriculum used in your classroom.
  - Is it inclusive or representative of all students in your classroom?
  - Regardless of your student population, is there a strong presence of literary and academic contributions of people of color?
  - From what point in history or from what perspectives are works/readings from or about people of color coming from? (i.e., when teaching African American history, are you starting with slave narratives only? Or when discussing famous Mexican leaders, do you refer only to Cesar Chavez? When discussing Christopher Columbus, is there discussion about the indigenous people who occupied the Americas long before Columbus?)
  - Does your curriculum ensure that you are teaching youth to be socially conscious beings?
  - Does your curriculum meet the educational needs and wants of all students in your class?
  - Who has the most creative oversight in the development of new curriculum?

- Reconsider prevailing systems of thought.
  - Interrogate policies and practices with a lens of equity. Look specifically at grading practices, homework policies, policies on retaking assessments, consequences for misbehavior, and what constitutes a "good student."
  - Conduct a mini-audit for each practice above. Ask yourself: Are students faring the same under my current practices?
  - Challenge yourself to rethink the practices you find may be placing some students at a disadvantage and others at an unfair advantage.

- Evaluate your concept of fairness.
    - Get to the root of what societal constructs you are basing your concept of what is ethical, fair, and just.
    - Learn about different ways people view and understand what is ethical, fair, and just.
    - Find examples in the United States where what is legal is not always ethical, and what is ethical is not always legal. Do these types of contradictions take place inside your classroom? If so, who do these contradictions hurt most?
    - Resist treating students the same and work to see students as individuals with individual needs.

Beyond Schooling to Educating

Being an abolitionist teacher who uses antiracist curriculum and pedagogical practices is vital to the transition from teaching within the status quo to one where students are being liberated and empowered through information.

In her book, *Black Appetite. White Food*, Jamila Lyiscott suggests that antiracist pedagogy requires teachers to teach their curriculum in a way that models how to "take action against the ideologies, institutional practices, and interpersonal reinforcements that have embedded themselves into [the] consciousness" (2019, p. 79) of each American-born student. An antiracist teacher chooses to use antiracist pedagogy such as culturally relevant education (Ladson-Billings, 1995), culturally responsive teaching theory (Gay, 2002), or the historically responsive literacy framework (Muhammad, 2020) to re-invigorate student minds and prevent students from blindly accepting traditional curriculum. Instead, students of antiracist educators are taught to "affirm their cultural identity, and develop critical perspectives that challenge inequities that schools and other institutions perpetuate" (Ladson-Billings, 1995).

To do this work with integrity, a teacher intent on becoming an antiracist and abolitionist educator must also seek to learn his or her own cultural and ethnic ways of knowing and being. Antiracist educators must also seek out historical truths and root causes of systemic oppression, and take a journey of self-reflection. Though the journey of self-reflection is not an easy one, Lyiscott, postulates that "Social justice requires personal wellness. Public impact requires private introspection" (2019). Uncomfortable as the journey through introspection and self-reflection may be, the impact that educators can have on the re-education of society far outweigh the struggles. Your introspection and self-reflection work should include the following:

- Identify your own ideologies and beliefs.
- Get in a state of readiness to accept hard truth about your own implicit biases.
  - Consider conducting an "archeology of self" and engage on a journey of self-reflection.
  - Engage in mindfulness or meditation practice.
- Take a test to survey implicit bias. A great place to start is Harvard's Implicit Association Test (IAT; https://implicit.harvard.edu/implicit/takeatest.html).
- Have a colleague observe a lesson to help call out your implicit biases. Check for:
  - Types of questions asked of traditionally *marginalized groups* (one-word questions eliciting one-word answers)
  - Types of questions being asked of *white students* (usually higher-order thinking)
- Observer's perceptions of nonquantifiable data, or *culture-reinforcing data.*
  - How many personal questions/positive comments does the teacher ask of the students? (e.g., How is your family? How is your mom? Nice shoes. I like your outfit. You look happy today! You look sad today, what is going on? Do you have a game today?)
  - How many negative questions/negative comments does the teacher ask of the students? (e.g.,. Are we going to have a better day today? I heard you got in trouble in Ms. X's class. Did you turn in your homework? Pull your pants up. You look upset today, I hope you can keep it together in class.)

- What type of comments, questions, or personal touch points is the teacher offering to *marginalized, female students*? *Marginalized, male students?*
- What types of comments, questions or personal touch points is the teacher offering to *white, female students? White, male students?*

From Well Intentioned to Well Done

Jamila Lyiscott explains that "some of the most deeply problematic issues of inequity within the field of education are sustained by well-meaning people embracing progressive politics without intentional frameworks of self-reflection to guide their praxis in a healthy direction" (2019, p. 14). Lyiscott furthers this idea by asking, "How in the world are you going to address the sociopolitical systemic magnitude of racial injustice without deep self-awareness of how to navigate your own personal struggles?" (p. 14).

This concept can also explain why "most forms of dialogue, diversity training, and other cognitive interventions are going to have little effect on [one's] reflexive fear responses" (Menakem, 2017, p. 91). What this means is that until educators spend enough time in deep reflection, getting in tune with their bodily sensations, they cannot get to the root of their *fear responses*, or the body's noncognitive way of responding to the places or people that scare us.

Thus, educators must be "honest about [our] private and personal stuff" (Lyiscott, 2019, p. 16). They must be able to see how their "stuff," such as biases, traumas, and experiences, intersect with their social identities (i.e., race, class, gender, language,) and how those social identities "map themselves onto [their] motivation, habits, and behaviors. Behaviors that lead [them] to the point of having the best intentions for changing the course of racial justice but the worst approach" (Lyiscott, 2019, p. 16).

Educators can immerse themselves in research to build frameworks of self-reflection and to guide praxis. Suggested readings include:

- *Black Appetite White Food* by Jamila Lyiscott
- *For White Folks Who Teach in the Hood . . . and the Rest of Y'all Too* by Christopher Emdin
- *We Want To Do More Than Survive* by Bettina Love
- *Culturally Responsive Teaching and the Brain* by Zaretta Hammond
- *Cultivating Genius* by Gholdy Muhammad
- *Other People's Children* by Lisa Delpit
- *White Fragility* by Robin DiAngelo
- *How to Be an Antiracist* by Ibram X. Kendi
- Articles on critical race theory (many authors)
- Articles on critical hip-hop pedagogy (Chris Emdin, Bettina Love, Jamila Lyiscott, etc.)

Elementary and secondary teachers might revisit their notion of classroom rules and consequences. Identify to what extent your classroom rules promote racist and discriminatory practices. For example, consider the task of *raising your hand to speak*. Is this practice in tune with the cultural practices of your students? Why or why not? Is it more in line with western European/individualistic practices of communication where there is a strong belief in "I speak, you speak"? Or is your rule in alignment with the call-and-response style similar to non–western European, collectivist cultures?

Teachers should enhance their knowledge and understanding of their noncognitive responses by developing a mindfulness or meditation practice. Suggested readings include:

- *Search Inside Yourself* by Chade Meng Tan
- *My Grandmother's Hands: Racialized Trauma and the Pathways to Mending Our Hearts and Bodies* by Resmaa Menakem
- *The Places That Scare You* by Pema Chodron

Be Intentional about the Unintentional

Searching inside ourselves with the intention of becoming aware of "the shifting realities of our mental health, family dysfunction, triggers, traumas, and all of the heavy things that impact how we show up to our classroom" (Lyiscott,

2019, p, 13) will prove helpful in many ways. It will also prove helpful in identifying the types of students our bodies are innately more prone to loving.

Processing the way our bodies react toward some bodies versus others plays a central role in dismantling racism and discrimination in classrooms. In his book, *My Grandmother's Hands: Racialized Trauma and the Pathway to Mending our Hearts and Bodies*, author Resmaa Menakem (2017) explains that recent findings in psychobiology have found that our deepest emotions—love, fear, anger, dread, grief, sorrow, and hopelessness—are visceral. The part of the brain where these visceral reactions occur is "a complex system of nerves [that] connect the brainstem, pharynx, heart, lungs, stomach, gut, and spine" (Menakem, 2017, p. 5). Serving as part of this complex set of nerves is the vagus nerve, a nerve directly "connected to the part of our brain that doesn't use cognition or reasoning as its primary tool for navigating the world" (p. 5).

Despite not intentionally *feeling some kind of way* toward different groups of students, the non-thinking brain takes over in this respect. In fact, when meeting an unfamiliar person, such as a new student, our body scans for hundreds of clues to determine if we can "relax in recognition or constrict in self-protection" (Menakem, 2017, p. 93). Without being cognizant of these processes, the brain is scanning the other individual's size, posture, clothing, and speed of approach; what the body is saying or doing; the vibrations it seems to be giving out; the expression on the person's face; and so on. A shortcut that the "brain uses to make this determination is asking, *how closely does this body match mine?*" (p. 93).

Menakem offers that it is "no surprise, then, that many white bodies relax when they encounter other unfamiliar white bodies, but constrict when they encounter unknown Black ones" (2017, p. 94). With approximately 79.3% of U.S. public school teachers being white, one can assume that not all have come to know how to love the approximate 55% non-white students in the American public education system (National Center for Education Statistics [NCES], 2020) because their bodies unknowingly recognize them as unfamiliar.

In the same way, the approximate 20% of non-white teachers may not know how to love the approximate 49% of white students (NCES, 2020) in their classrooms, for the same reason. These findings indicate that without an awareness of one's central emotions and how individuals come to be socialized into the norms and values that have scripted one's life, there is no way to rewire the brain to blindly love all students.

So, as an educator, what can you do? First, identify your "favorite" student(s) and your "least favorite" student(s) in each class.

- What are the common characteristics among the "favorite" students?
- Describe the types of interactions you have with these students. What questions are you asking them? How frequently do you engage in positive interactions with these students?
- What are the common characteristics among the "least favorite" students?
- Reflect on the types of interactions you are having with these students. What questions are you asking them? How frequently do you engage in positive interactions with these students?
- Then, challenge yourself to apply those same practices/interactions used with your "favorite" students to the students who are *not your favorites*.

Second, identify students in your zone of self-efficacy (McKenzie & Lozano, 2008).

- On a sheet of paper, draw a circle no more than 3–4 inches in diameter.
- Using your class roster, write the names of the students who are the "easiest to teach" in the center of the circle.
- Write the names of students left out of the "inner circle" on the outside of the circle. Those students whom are placed inside the circle are within your "zone of self-efficacy," which means that you are most comfortable

teaching those students. You are not as comfortable teaching those students who are outside of the circle.
- Review who is in the inside and outside of your circle:
  - Count how many males and females are listed inside the circle. Repeat the process for those outside the circle.
  - Take note of the ethnic backgrounds of the students listed inside the circle. Repeat the process for students outside of the circle.
  - Take note of the socioeconomic levels of those inside your circle and those outside your circle.
  - Take note of how many English learners are inside your circle compared to those whose names are on the outside.
  - Challenge yourself to find ways to bring all students who are listed on the "outside" of your "zone of self-efficacy" to the inside of your circle.

Love Blindly; Don't Be Color-Blind

The core tenet of *bodhichitta* is to blindly and openly love each human who comes onto one's path. To blindly and openly love each student who walks through the door is therefore the main objective when striving to become a Bodhi-teacha. To be clear, educators should not become *color blind*, as this encompasses racial erasure, and is the antithesis of loving blindly.

Instead, educators should aim to look at their students through a biological antiracist lens, a term Ibram X. Kendi, author of *How to Be an Antiracist* (2019) describes as the "idea that the races are meaningfully the same in their biology and that there are no genetic racial differences" (p. 44). Kendi's definition recognizes race as a non-factor. This is an important piece of information when viewing and loving students. If educators can look at students through this biological antiracist lens, then they can begin to see students through the lens of the *bodhichitta* concept of form.

This *bodhichitta* concept of form is described as something that just "*is* before we project our concepts on it. It is the original state of *what is here*, the colorful, vivid, impressive, dramatic, aesthetic qualities that exists in every situation. These things are *what is* and they are all in one sense the same: they are all forms" (Trungpa, 2002). By looking at students through this lens of "form" and not allowing western forms or social constructs to do the job of defining who our students are for us, we can begin to see the colorful, impressive, dramatic, aesthetic qualities that exists within each of our students. This act can bring us closer to dismantling racism, discrimination, and white supremacy.

The brand of patience cultivated by one who practices *bodhichitta* is that of fearlessness of new situations. Nothing can surprise the *bodhisattva*, or one who practices *bodhichitta*. "Whatever comes—be it destructive, chaotic, creative, welcoming, or inviting—the *bodhisattva* is never disturbed, never shocked, because he is aware of the space between the situation and himself" (Trungpa, 2002, p. 175). With time and effort, teachers too, can develop this brand of patience, so that no matter what kind of students they have in class, they can hold space for these students, and allow them to be their full selves. Teachers can love them in whatever form they are. Developing this level of patience makes room for the type of generosity prescribed by *bodhichitta*.

Generosity, by *bodhichitta* standards, is "a willingness to give, to open without philosophical or pious or religious motives, just simply doing what is required at any moment in any situation" (Trungpa, 2002, p. 171). Consider that the most effective teachers are the ones generous enough and willing to do whatever is required to help their students feel and be successful in class. When a teacher is willing to do whatever it takes to teach students, not only is it impossible for students to become bored, but it shows students the lengths that caring adults are willing to go to in order to see them rise!

The wonderful thing about developing *bodhichitta*-like practices as an educator is that "one never sees situations as uninteresting or stagnant at all, because the [Bodhi-teacha's] view of life is extremely open-minded, and intensely interested. She sees situations from a panoramic point of view and therefore takes a great deal of interest in life as it is" (Trungpa, 2002, p. 178). Teachers who share this view always enjoy their jobs, despite having challenging days. This happens because they truly and wholeheartedly enjoy working with their students. They also take in each day, as they take in each student—how it comes, in whatever form it comes, loving with no judgment.

Here's what YOU can do to become a Bodhi-teacha:

- Begin a mindfulness awareness practice. This cultivates loving kindness and compassion, the qualities of *bodhichitta*. It gives a way to move closer to one's thoughts and emotions and to get in touch with one's bodies. Mindfulness practice also helps to develop steadfastness, a characteristic required when practicing anti-racism and abolitionist teaching.
- Leave any ego outside the classroom door by remembering that educators are not separate from their students. Both teacher and student are learners, and therefore what is being taught in the classroom is co-constructed and always fluid.
- Learn to accept yourself just as you are and begin a direct relationship with who you are. The more you accept yourself and work directly with all of your "good parts and bad parts," the faster you can do the same with your students.
- Learn to see students just as they are, in whatever form they come. When you can see students for the gifts they have, it gives them permission to see themselves in that same light.

- Develop *equanimity* or the ability to stay calm and maintain your composure and evenness of temper, especially in a difficult situation. (No teacher wants their freak-out uploaded to social media.) In all seriousness, if you *do* end up thinking about it like this, you will eventually learn to stay calm under any heightened situation in your class.

Recognize that to love every student in the class means to know, validate, and affirm each of them. Teachers can involve students in collective and personal inquiry/exploration of student cultures/identities. For example, the teacher of a middle school social studies class could create a beginning-of-year activity such as a "gallery walk" where students:

- Identify their surface culture through photos and other items.
- Discuss their deeper identities by exploring how and why their people came to live in the United States.
- Research the treatment of their people upon arrival to the United States.
- Analyze their people within the current sociopolitical context of their communities, society, and the world.

Teachers can also ask students to write autobiographies, graphic novels, and/or personal narratives:

- Be willing to share your story first.
- Create a space where students want to share with you and each other.
- Invite students to read each other's stories.
- Invite families and the community to a "reading" of your students' autobiographies as a way to affirm, validate, and better understand your students and for students to better understand each other.

Make a list of common statements or labels that are made or formed about students, specifically marginalized students. Then challenge the biases behind them. Instead, think about each student as being indigenous to your classroom.

- Question statements such as:
  - "Black kids don't value education."
  - "Mexican families never show up on time."
  - "Asian kids are good at math."
  - "Girls are more organized than boys."
  - "Poor people don't value education."
- Challenge labels such as:
  - "at risk"
  - "defiant"
  - "disadvantaged"
  - "non-readers"
  - "struggling"
  - "English learner"

Other actions YOU can take inside and out of the classroom:

- Revisit your perspectives on traditional classroom discipline. Ask yourself:
  - What would happen to your classroom environment if you never sent a student out of the class for misbehavior?
  - What would it mean if all behavior problems were solved in your classroom?
  - Could this practice create an environment where students feel safer under your care?
  - Could the act of not kicking out a student reset how they view themselves?

- Instead of students viewing themselves as "nuisances" in the environment, in need of removal, could they instead begin to see themselves as "native" to the environment and in need of extra care?
- Have you ever thought that doing your best to solve discipline issues in your classroom gains respect from students? After all, in the eyes of many students, whoever solves the problem gains the respect.

• Seek to become the mental health first responder in your classroom by learning about trauma and by becoming certified in Mental Health First Aid.

- Seek Trauma-Informed Teaching professional development through your district, county office of education, area behavioral health centers, or professional education organizations.
- Sign up for Mental Health First Aid training through a county or state health organization.
- Research trauma, healing, mental health, and the brain.

• Separate students from the behaviors they exhibit.

- Seek to understand each student's behavior patterns before punishing misbehavior.
- Learn to see student behavior as a form of communication, so that if a student is behaving a certain way, it is seen as attempting to communicate an unmet need.
- Uncover the types of activities, noises, or distractions that may be triggering a student's adverse behaviors and seek to correct the "things" first, not the student.

- Love the parents too. Even the angry ones.
    - Remember that at the end of the day, all people want to be loved and happy, even disgruntled parents.
    - Rather than seeing angry parents as problems, a teacher can view these parents as people who love their child so much that they came to school/emailed you to passionately advocate for the child.
    - Apologize to the parent and thank them for visiting you. Then work together to come up with a game plan to advance the student you both love.

Are You for Real about This Bodhi-Teacha Stuff?

Yes. There is no denying the urgency in the fight against racism, discrimination, and educational inequalities. And there is no denying that the strength of pure love is stronger than the hate that maintains these oppressive systems. So if being a "Bodhi-teacha" means teaching with a weapon stronger than these oppressive systems; *I'm down*. In support of those creating a way through this heavy battle is Bettina Love, who says that "there is no one way to be an abolitionist teacher. Some teachers will create a homeplace for their students . . . some will protest in the streets . . . some will restore justice in their classrooms . . . some will create justice-centered curriculums and teaching" (2019), and some will study the path of a *bodhichitta* warrior. But no matter the pathway *you* choose or the actions *you* choose to take, do it purely out of love for your students and their humanity. The students' well-being is at stake.

READER TAKEAWAYS

- Becoming familiar with your own ideologies and belief systems is vital to the work of antiracist and abolitionist teaching.
- Educational equity needs to be thought of as an "action" and not simply as an idea.
- Antiracist and abolitionist teaching pedagogies are the "action" steps needed to achieve equitable education.
- Unless individuals are in tune with their bodies, the "non-thinking" brain may trigger one's body to respond adversely toward those

whom one is not familiar. This could potentially harm relationship-building with students.
- Conduct regular equity audits on your grading practices, curriculum, rules, policies, cultural climate, etc.
- Beginning a mindfulness awareness practice will help you tune into your body and will help you cultivate compassion and love.
- To love every student in your class means to know, validate, and affirm each of them.

REFERENCES

Gay, G. (2002). Preparing for culturally responsive teaching. *Journal of Teacher Education, 53*(2), 106–116.

Kendi, I. (2019). *How to be an antiracist*. One World Press.

Ladson-Billings, G. (1995). Toward a theory of culturally relevant pedagogy. *American Educational Research Journal, 32*(3), 465–491.

Ladson-Billings, G. (2014). Culturally relevant pedagogy 2.0: Aka the remix. *Harvard Educational Review, 84*(1), 74–84.

Love, B. (2019). *We want to do more than survive: Abolitionist teaching and the pursuit of educational freedom*. Beacon Press.

Lyiscott, J. (2019). *Black appetite. white food: Issues of race, voice, and justice within and beyond the classroom*. Routledge.

McKenzie, K., & Lozano, R. (2008). Teachers' zone of self-efficacy: Which students get included, which students get excluded, and more importantly, why. *National Journal of Urban Education and Practice, (1)*4, 372–384.

Menakem, R. (2017). *My grandmother's hands: Racialized trauma and the pathways to mending our hearts and bodies*. Central Recovery Press.

Muhammad, G. (2020). *Cultivating genius: An equity framework for culturally and historically responsive literacy*. Scholastic.

National Center for Education Statistics. (2020, May). *Characteristics of Public School Teachers*. https://nces.ed.gov/programs/coe/pdf/2021/clr_508c.pdf

Noguera, P. (2020, December 11). *Where the promise of the American dream falls short in schools* [Video]. Edutopia. https://www.edutopia.org/video/where-promise-americandream-falls-short-schools

Rinpoche, L. (2019). *Bodhichitta practice for a meaningful life*. Wisdom Publications.

Trungpa, C. (2002). *Cutting through spiritual materialism*. Shambhala Press.

SEVEN

The Newcomer Student Experience

Opportunities to Empower, Engage, and Advocate for Immigrant Students

Lindsey Bird

We can, whenever and wherever we choose, successfully teach all children whose schooling is of interest to us. We already know more than we need to do that. Whether or not we do it must finally depend on how we feel about the fact that we haven't so far.

—Ron Edmondspi

EXPECTED LEARNING OUTCOMES

- Readers will gain insight into the cultural competencies and best practices that welcome students and families new to the country into the school system.
- Readers will be provided specific examples of how to identify, engage, empower, and accelerate language acquisition and self-efficacy for newcomer English learners.
- Readers will understand the need for both quantitative and qualitative data and how that information can be used to provide targeted support for diverse English learner profiles within the school setting.

WHAT I KNOW

Students learning English as a second language are a demographic to whom schools are legally required to provide additional services and support along their journey of mastering our nation's primary language and striving for the literacy and numeracy needed to have all of life's options at their fingertips upon high school graduation. And rightfully so, considering proficiency in English is often a gatekeeper to fulfilling the modern American Dream. Yet the label "English learner" embodies so much more diversity and complexity than the classification leads an educator to initially believe. It is vital that teachers don't settle for that simplistic label as the only indicator of specific student needs.

Asking questions is the best way to honor the variety of experiences, in addition to both academic and linguistic needs, within the English learner student population. These should include:

- What is the student's primary language?
- Is the student literate in their primary language?
- Might there also be a secondary language spoken within the home?
- What is the student's formal education experience in the primary language?
- Does the student have any prior experience or education in English?

Sure, the answers to those questions can help an educator tailor English language acquisition around individual needs. But aren't students more than their *language* ability, regardless of the language? To fully meet the needs of the English learner population, the education system—as well as those employed by it—must consider the whole child. In doing so, further questions include, but are not limited to:

- Has the student spent most or all of their life in the United States speaking a language other than English at home?
- How many years has the student spent in the U.S. school system?
- Is the student's verbal English ability at par with their academic English ability?
- Does the student have any formal education in their primary language?
- Does the student have a history of academic success?
- Is the student new to the United States?

- If so, what conditions caused the student to leave their native land?

This chapter will be dedicated to the nuances of those situations where the answer to the last question is "yes, the student is a newly arrived immigrant/refugee/asylum seeker." While the whole child should always be considered regardless of demographic labels assigned by the school or school system, the needs of newcomers are often so unique and complex that they rarely get consideration. As educators, and as people, it is reasonable to state that when it comes to the needs of newcomers, staff and faculty simply don't know what they don't know. The hope is the insight provided here will pave a road to empathy and inquiry that leads to a better school experience for the newcomer student and teacher alike.

WHAT YOU NEED TO KNOW

In any educational setting, the acknowledgement that the English learner student population has differing needs based on more than pure language ability is foundational. By properly identifying a student as a newcomer, and then addressing the environmental and emotional layers that accompany that reality, a school has a much greater chance of accelerating comfort, self-efficacy and, inevitably, language development and content mastery.

Translation

Students new to the United States often have their introduction to the public school system during the enrollment process. The assumption is that the experience is shared by the immediate family unit, but it is important to realize that a significant portion of newcomer students do not reside with their parent(s). Staff development around the cultural competencies that can make the enrollment experience as supportive and welcoming as possible could be the building blocks of a student's sense of belonging in the school.

Without cutting corners on legal and compliance requirements, it is possible to approach this often confusing and overwhelming process as an opportunity to encourage the student and their guardians alike to ask the questions essential to success. If the student is not residing with their immediate family unit, it is common for the basic knowledge and forms needed during enrollment to be unknown or missing, making staff development around cultural competency as important for those involved in this process as it is for the teachers who will be welcoming the student to their classrooms.

The first step to ensure enrollment goes smoothly is having as many documents translated into the primary languages of the community as possible. While a 2015 joint memo from the U.S. Department of Justice and the U.S. Department of Education (U.S. Department of Justice/U.S. Department of Education, 2015b) was issued reminding schools and districts of their civil rights obligation to communicate with limited English proficient parents and guardians in their primary language, the local implementation of that goal often lags behind community needs.

The memo also reminds those working in any capacity within public education that relying on translation or interpretation from the child, siblings, other students, or untrained school staff is not acceptable. The document goes on to identify areas in which families should be provided appropriate primary language access, including but not limited to:

- Registration and enrollment in school and school programs
- Language assistance programs
- Report cards
- Student discipline policies and procedures
- Parent-teacher conferences
- Grievance procedures and notices of nondiscrimination

Meaningful access to this vital information in a language the parent or guardian understands, upon enrollment and throughout the overall experience within the public school setting, is a lifeline to student success. State and local policies often place mandates on primary language access *only* if the percentages of native speakers of a specific language hit a certain threshold, yet the spirit behind the recommendations are not bolstered or diluted by the abundance (or lack thereof) of any one specific language.

With or without a policy or legal decree, the need for proper translation is something a school district should dedicate resources toward as an investment in the potential of the children of those not literate in English. This often means forging relationships with those in the community who work outside the silo of education, but have a keen awareness and knowledge of the ever-changing demographics of the region. For example, refugee resettlement agencies, nonprofits serving immigrant communities, community service agencies under the county's umbrella of health and social services, and faith-based community outreach networks are all ways for a school district to keep an ear to the ground regarding evolving community linguistic needs.

In addition, when a school does not have the internal capacity to translate or interpret documents into the language(s) of the non-English-speaking community, these external relationships do more than build bridges of understanding. They also serve as an opportunity for the efficient use of highly skilled and specific linguistic resources, a way in which the education system can be proactive rather than reactive to community need, and serve as a collaborative partnership in identifying and addressing the wrap-around services that students and families new to our nation too often go without.

State and national government entities often have resources to assist schools and districts in meeting the primary language needs of their community, either on staff or on a contractual basis. Schools should make every meaningful effort to ensure that the enrollment process includes primary language access, even if the primary language is not one common to the community.

Cultural Competency

Providing documents and information to parents and guardians in their primary language is a legal and moral obligation of the public school system, but that access is for nothing if it is not accompanied with a culturally competent staff. This can be as basic as the *body language* of all faculty and staff being warm and welcoming when unable to communicate in spoken language, to the specific cultural nuances of the families being served and how that knowledge could forge trust and acceptance rather than misunderstandings and division.

There must be ongoing intention behind a culturally competent and responsive faculty and staff, which includes professional development opportunities, a mission and vision that honor diversity, and site- and district-level leadership that model and invest in public education's obligation to meet the ever-changing needs of those they serve. The mutual understanding that access to quality education is the foundation to the creation and execution of the American Dream should be the North Star guiding schools through the challenges of serving students and families of different linguistic, cultural, educational, behavioral, and generational traditions.

In addition to having cultural and linguistic sensitivity, it is also important that schools adjust to the variety of educational histories that students and families new to the United States might potentially bring. For example, there should not be an assumption that a parent, guardian, or student is literate in their primary language.

For a variety of reasons, many families new to the country arrive with little to no literacy in their primary language, regardless of the age at which they arrive, leaving some traditional methods of communication through translated documents or technology-based resources ineffective. Having both the awareness and patience to anticipate situations like this can provide the empathy and compassion necessary to make the experience rewarding for all parties involved.

For students arriving with gaps in their formal education, or in some cases with no formal education at all, schools must be willing and able to tackle two tasks simultaneously: provide the student with English language acquisition, *and* provide a scaffolded academic program that gives the foundational knowledge and skills necessary to access grade-level content as rapidly as possible (U.S. Department of Justice/U.S. Department of Education, 2015a). In this situation, the older the student is at the time of enrollment, the more intentional the school needs to be in addressing the disconnect between the student's current abilities and the linguistic and academic skills to reasonably engage in a grade-level mainstream course.

For example, a 17-year-old refugee from Syria who has yet to master the Roman alphabet and has not been to school in six years would not have *reasonable* access to a U.S. history course. Should a school place that student there anyway because "all juniors take U.S. history," or should accommodations for acceleration and access be made? While the answer to that question is different at every school, it is beneficial to break out of the status quo mentality and explore equitable options to support students in such a scenario.

Age

It is commonly accepted that students learn to read in kindergarten through roughly third grade, and then *read to learn* after that, leaving primary-grade educators the task of providing grade-level literacy to their English learners and native English speakers alike. So what happens when a newcomer student enrolls in an American school at a grade level where literacy in English is not only assumed, but is the gatekeeper to access mainstream content? Here is where schools must be keenly aware that the linguistic and academic needs of the long-term English learners will diverge from the needs of the newcomers, with the intent of providing rigor, support, and access to both.

This is also where cultural competency, quantitative and qualitative data, and a proactive approach can engage newcomer students while honoring the diverse assets each individual brings upon arrival. For example, do all newcomers who test as "beginners" to the English language have the same academic abilities or educational experiences? Of course not. All states require a home language survey, as prescribed by federal policy, which begins with the English learner identification process.

Too often, the results of that initial English proficiency benchmark predict the overall scope of the student's academic pathway. This begs the question: are all English learners at the beginning phases of English acquisition the same? Although we instinctively know the answer to that question is no, so often those students are provided identical paths, limiting opportunities for both support and growth.

This is why the age of the student, in addition to *multiple quantitative and qualitative data points*, should not only guide student placement, but possibly influence course offerings at the school.

Quantitative Data

The mandated English proficiency assessment only gives a school one narrow insight into a student's overall ability. To properly place and accelerate newcomers, especially those who arrive in U.S. schools at the fourth-grade or later, additional data points should be incorporated into the enrollment process. These include, but are not limited to:

- A writing sample in the student's primary language (when supported by bilingual faculty able to assign a rubric-generated score)
- A writing sample in English using the same prompt as the primary language assessment
- A grade level–appropriate math assessment with written instructions provided in the student's primary language

- Culturally responsive analysis of quantitative data provided by student records from the native or secondary nation

Through these additional resources of quantitative data, a school can get a much fuller picture of the assets the student arrives with, in addition to possible insight into age-appropriate content remediations that create a bridge to meaningful grade-level access. Whereas two students might score nearly identical on the initial English proficiency assessment, further insight typically reveals diverging foundational literacy and content area needs.

Even if the master schedule of a school cannot justify the creation of specialized language acquisition or content-area support classes, the information being passed on to the classroom teachers and support staff often proves invaluable.

Qualitative Data

Schools are typically measured in terms of the quantitative data they produce—standardized test scores, matriculation and graduation rates, and student success markers such as letter and citizenship grades. So, it is not surprising that those means of progress evaluation are often passed on as reasonable measures of individual student progress as well. Yet schools are tasked with meeting the needs of the whole child, needs that cannot be measured by analyzing scores and data alone.

In fact, those data points often reflect unmet needs outside the scope of academics as much as they measure academics itself. This is true for all students, but especially students new to the United States, our public school system, the English language, and occasionally the Roman alphabet.

While qualitative data about a student is typically optional and rooted in the trust and comfort a student has in their respective school environment, if obtained, it can lead to potentially life-changing results. In addition to including an enrollment survey as part of the onboarding process, which often leads to incomplete responses or answers not applicable to the student's educational plan, it is best to identify opportunities to garner this more personal information in response to intentional and spontaneous opportunities after a relationship with the student has been established.

Visual cues can plant seeds of trust and acceptance, which often help relationships form sooner, such as international flags representing the diversity of the community, a world map identifying the number of students from a particular country, in addition to materials being translated into the student's primary language. All illustrate a sense of belonging.

If a school employs primary-language or English writing samples as part of the enrollment assessment, the wording of the prompt could also open a door of insight into information needed to truly meet the needs of the whole child. Stories of successes and failures in prior educational experiences, goals for the future, or personal anecdotes can all provide great insight into addressing possible trauma, identifying effective teaching strategies, designing a class schedule aimed at optimal motivation, and plugging the student into appropriate supports or extracurricular opportunities on campus. In this case, the samples provide both quantitative and qualitative data, establishing a benchmark for academic growth and a peek inside the newcomer as a person.

When this type of data can be collected upon enrollment, via formative assessment or during an in-class assignment or discussion, it is optimized when the team of faculty and staff in charge of English learner student success are made aware of the information. Some student data programs allow for notes to be digitally entered to track qualitative data gathered or pertinent observations made, while some teams must rely on informal communication or a structured collaboration process for the opportunity to share information intended to optimize student success and empowerment.

Vital qualitative data can also be garnered from in-class assignments intended to elicit personal connections within the classroom, such as icebreakers, "get to know you" presentations, graphic novels written and illustrated about firsthand student experiences, and a multitude of team-building projects that focus on building awareness and community regardless of course content. While pacing guides and standardized tests often encourage teachers to shy away from this use of valuable class time, in the end the understanding built among peers and inclusion of newcomers *always* pays off.

Acceleration Opportunity

In addition to the mandated annual state assessments, schools that build the capacity to include quantitative and qualitative data opportunities for newcomers should also circle back to those benchmarks as a means to measure growth over the course of the school year. This provides both the student and teachers an opportunity to see the fruits of their labor, in addition to providing data that could support the subjective observations of teachers and support staff.

If the school's master schedule includes elective and content-specific newcomer support classes, highly encouraged for schools with significant numbers of newcomers whose initial assets are disconnected from the skills needed for meaningful access to grade-level curriculum, students should not be forced to remain in those sections if mid-year data shows the growth to succeed in a mainstream environment. That nuance shifts the intention of the specialized courses from segregation to *acceleration*, providing the foundational skills needed for mainstream success without the hindrance of not being able to test or opt out of these recommended (but optional) supports.

Providing newcomers access to the specific content, courses, and foundational skills that translate to mainstream success must be implemented with clearly defined roles for student case management. Depending on local district policy, especially at the high school level, these opportunities for acceleration can lead to a student being "off track" for matriculation or graduation. By allowing students to mainstream mid-year, students are able to access the rigor that matches their ambitions, but also leaves room for atypical graduation planning in comparison to fully mainstreamed peers.

The extra back-office work that newcomer acceleration opportunities provide is far outweighed by the life-changing self-efficacy that can empower newcomers, but it must be done with conviction and commitment from all levels of the school system. National data clearly show that students who arrive in the United States as teenagers, especially those with truncated formal education, are some of the most *at-risk* English learners within the system. Yet if the school system approaches them with empathy, coupled with a deep belief in their unlimited potential, this portion of the English learner demographic can quickly be redefined as *at-promise*.

Imagine being a young woman born and raised in a Taliban-controlled village in Pakistan, denied all opportunity for literacy in your spoken language; signing your name on enrollment documents at your new U.S. school was the first time you picked up a pencil. Students like this exist throughout our nation. Exploring ways to honor their journey, while illuminating the possibilities education can provide them in their new nation, is not just an investment in worthy individuals, but an investment in the spirit of the American Dream.

Local Education Policy

Equity cannot be a buzzword limited to the expectations a school district places on its classroom teachers. Equity should be employed from top to bottom, from the principal's office to the boardroom—and most importantly, in district policy. The demands being placed on educators to close achievement gaps, rethink classroom management, be aware of implicit bias, and integrate technology into daily routines have educators feeling as if the weight of the nation is on their shoulders.

Communities who truly want to experience a renaissance within local public education must realize that all layers of the system must be examined for innovation opportunities, especially when exploring ways to better serve newcomers. Communities need to hold more than just classroom teachers responsible for the reinvention needed to transform public education.

Thinking back to the Pakistani student described above and her need for equitable access, it is important to remember that a 17-year-old who is just learning how to use a pencil is going to need more than a specialized course or curriculum. The primary ingredient that student would need for a reasonable opportunity at literacy and self-reliance is *time*. While federal Title III policy offers schools and districts the opportunity to extend access to education for newcomer students through age 21, it is local policy that dictates if and how that is applied.

Some districts have specific newcomer policies embedded within their English learner master plan, providing equitable opportunity for students who arrive in U.S. schools at the secondary level, but most do not. This is where the line between equity and equality becomes fuzzy.

Is articulating policies specifically for newcomers giving them an *advantage* others do not have? While some fervently answer yes, the data suggests that sticking to the antiquated notion that what we do for one, we must do for all, has gotten us to a place where, decade after decade, the same student demographics continually slip through the cracks. Moreover, if a policy proves to provide equity and access to newcomers, why not explore expanding it to more students?

There truly is no "harm" in blazing an equitable pathway for immigrant, refugee, and asylum-seeking students who join our communities as teens, especially when their success sets the tone for their families and generations to come.

In addition to offering some newcomers the option of more time within the school system, districts can also be innovative in addressing secondary newcomer needs from a more holistic perspective. For example, if the Pakistani 17-year-old happens to be one of just a few newcomers with both language acquisition and content remediation needs, is it truly feasible to expect a site to invest time and resources for specialized courses and curriculum? Since the answer to that question is overwhelmingly no, districts must brainstorm ways to meet newcomer community needs on a grander scale.

For larger districts with more than one high school campus, consolidating newcomers to one site might provide the number of students to justify an investment in specific newcomer needs. Other potential benefits of this model include providing multiple levels of language acquisition and scaffolded content courses to increase engagement and rigor, in addition to the opportunity for newcomers to access the mainstream courses in the comprehensive master schedule as warranted.

What's wrong with a Mandarin-speaking student mastering the foundation of the English language while simultaneously taking AP calculus? Nothing. In fact, therein lies the beauty of placing newcomer programs and pathways within a comprehensive site. Newcomer families should have options and access, just like their native-born counterparts.

Other districts have found a separate campus, completely dedicated to the academic and cultural needs of newcomers, is a better fit for their respective communities. Either way, districts that honor the reality that the needs of secondary newcomer students are drastically different than their long-term English learner or native English-speaking peers, make clear their understanding of equity and their belief in the potential of these deserving at-promise immigrant, refugee, and asylum-seeking students.

WHAT YOU CAN DO

In the Classroom

Almost all institutions of public education have students new to the county and the English language enrolling throughout the academic school year. While some of the recommendations in this chapter might be aspirational for future enrollment procedures, professional development opportunities, curriculum adoption, or program offerings, what should teachers do if those services do not currently exist for newcomers in their classrooms? Below are a few suggestions for classroom strategies and advocacy opportunities:

- Always allow newcomers to access their funds of knowledge in their primary language through verbal, written, or technology-based translation.
- Educate classmates about the country and primary language of the newcomer and seize all opportunities to build cultural competency within your classroom environment.
- Decorate your classroom with visual cues to honor diversity.
- Pre-establish a cue for when the newcomer will be called on, such as pulling your ear or clasping your hand together.
- Always allow extra time for newcomers to process auditory input and produce verbal output.
- Establish classroom routines that encourage academic discussion prior to a called-on response to provide newcomers with exposure and practice to the English needed for participation.
- If available, ensure newcomers have access to additional support through bilingual paraprofessional support staff.
- Do not assume newcomer students know the U.S. school system and be willing to educate them as much as possible regarding your respective content area or course requirements.
- Incorporate multiple opportunities for newcomers to use the academic vocabulary in your content area through listening, speaking, reading, and writing.
- Allow newcomers to make multiple attempts toward mastery on assignments and assessments.
- Use the qualitative data you learn from newcomer students in your class to better design instruction, to create a culturally responsive

learning environment, and to share with colleagues to use in their efforts to serve the student.
- Ask administration for supplemental resources that accelerate English acquisition and remediate the grade-level skills needed for meaningful newcomer access to your curriculum.
- Be willing to seek knowledge and information about the country and culture from which the newcomer arrived and incorporate that into one-on-one conversations or class lessons.
- Advocate for newcomer needs in your classroom, at the site level, and be their voice when there are opportunities to influence the district to better meet their needs.

In the Community

At any grade or age, acknowledging the trauma of moving to a new country and enrolling in a foreign school as an act of bravery, and honoring it with empathy and belief in student potential, is all any newcomer parent or guardian could want for their child. Yet the ideas of empathy and belief also deserve actions—intentional actions, set forth through a plan of culturally competent and responsive policies, practices, and pedagogies. This requires not only cognitive awareness and determination, but an "all hands on deck" approach to ensure that the needs of newcomer students and families do not go unnoticed or underserved.

Most Americans have family tales of the first generation that arrived in this great nation, often poor and not speaking English, who rolled up their sleeves and were able to provide for their family. While continuing to applaud the determination and sacrifices of our ancestors, it is also worthwhile to point out that literacy and education play an even more vital role in the modern global economy than they did generations ago, placing weight on quality and equitable public education now more than ever.

Seeing our students as the adults they are destined to become promotes the sense of urgency needed to provide them with the tools to become the contributing, self-reliant community members they aim to be. National political rhetoric has recently eroded the notion that America is a "nation of immigrants," distracting our efforts to proactively creating the more perfect union the Founding Fathers challenged us to create.

Quality, accessible, and equitable education has always been the key to the American Dream. In fact, often it is institutional racism, implicit bias, and oppressive power structures that created the generational suffering rising to the surface of public conscientiousness. So it is vital that society, specifically the public education system, not perpetuate that cycle for those newly arrived to our nation.

While the details of what traditionally marginalized groups and newcomer students need in terms of content and curriculum might be different, the mindset and innovation necessary to better serve them is the same. Once educational institutions value the education of *all* children as much as they value the education of "their own," and take measurable actions to demonstrate their commitment to all children, we can rest assured that the newcomers who enter our schools today will not become the parents of students who illustrate the achievement gaps of tomorrow.

As educators, community members, and Americans, one thing *everyone* can do for our newcomer students and families is use our voice and our vote to honor their experience. Public education is local in all aspects, leaving engaged parents and citizens more opportunities for meaningful influence than most hot-button national topics.

If the expectation is for those within the education sector to honor the children of others as if they were their own, then all community members must also carry the needs of those children with them into meetings, conversations with elected trustees and, most importantly, on the ballot by voting for candidates who will comprise those boards. All children, but especially the children of those yet to know our language or the intricacies of our school system, should be in our hearts and minds as the public education system uplifts those most vulnerable in our communities by providing the hand up they needed to reach their full potential.

The power of parents and community is both a blessing and a curse in the long road toward equitable education, as too often those without influence and a voice have gone unheard and underserved. Being mindful of the communal value in educating the children of others is the first step in an improved educational system.

READER TAKEAWAYS

- The diversity of the English learner demographic requires attention to individual assets and needs.

- Students new to the U.S. school system who arrive at the fourth-grade level and beyond need targeted and specific pathways to grade-level English proficiency and content mastery.
- The older a student is upon arrival in the U.S. school system, the greater the potential disconnect between student assets and the foundational literacy skills and content knowledge needed for meaningful access to grade-level curriculum.
- School districts have the autonomy to develop and design community-based newcomer policies, procedures, course, and pathways.
- Empathy, cultural competency, and belief in student potential must be the guiding principles behind efforts to better serve the needs of newcomers.
- Quantitative and qualitative data must be collected upon enrollment and throughout each school year to best support and accelerate newcomers in their educational journey.
- Acknowledgement that in today's global economy and interconnected society, literacy in English is the gatekeeper of the modern American Dream.

REFERENCES

U.S. Department of Justice/U.S. Department of Education, Office for Civil Rights. (2015a). *Ensuring English learner students can participate meaningfully and equally in educational programs.* Author.

U.S. Department of Justice/U.S. Department of Education, Office for Civil Rights. (2015b). *Information for Limited English Proficient (LEP) parents and guardians and for schools and school districts that communicate with them.* Author.

EIGHT

Building Meaningful Student and Parent Relationships

Nicole Lonergan and Ryan Lonergan

> Children are not a distraction from more important work. They are the most important work.
>
> —C. S. Lewis

EXPECTED LEARNING OUTCOMES

- Readers will understand the importance of fostering positive student–teacher relationships.
- Readers will develop practical applications of ways to create and maintain strong relationships with their students.
- Readers will gain insight into the importance of and ways to communicate and build relationships with parents of their students.

WHAT WE KNOW

Every year, teachers are met with a set of new faces, and typically, given the current situation in American classrooms, teachers may meet anywhere between 150 and 175 new students (at the secondary level) if their classrooms are filled to capacity. For elementary teachers, a classroom at capacity may be between 30 and 35 students. It is no easy task to personally get to know the students, their learning styles, and how to best work with them—yet teachers step up to the challenge and do just that every year. Teachers do this because building strong, quality relationships with students is at the heart of effective teaching.

The importance of fostering positive relationships with students goes beyond impacting students' academic performance. In large part this is because "outside of their parents, children spend the majority of their time with educators, leaving teachers as the most influential nonparent adult relationship for children" (Hansen, 2018). Because teachers spend arguably more time with their students than other adults in their lives, they have the potential to influence them in major ways and, depending on the condition of the relationship, this influence can be either positive or negative. If teachers develop positive relationships with their students they have the ability to increase not only their students' academic performance and competency in the given subject area, but also their autonomy and ability to self-advocate—skills that will ultimately help them beyond the walls of our classrooms.

Furthermore, since students spend much of their time at school with teachers, it is also vital that teachers reach out to their students' parents as well. Parent outreach can seem daunting to teachers because it most often occurs for negative reasons, such as failing grades, bad behavior, or attendance issues. However, parent contact does not always have to be negative; in fact, parent outreach can and should be done for student successes and can also be used to strengthen classroom cultures.

Teacher-Student Relationships (TSRs)

The key to building positive and long-lasting relationships with students starts before they enter classrooms on the first day of school. How classrooms are set up, rules and procedures developed, and curriculum is prepared and designed are major contributing factors to teachers developing positive relationships with their students. Research indicates that positive teacher-student relationships (TSRs) can affect students' experiences during school in three primary areas: engagement, academic achievement, and student self-efficacy.

When teachers work to foster strong relationships with their students, they are more likely to have higher levels of classroom engagement. In fact, according to the study done by Roorda et al. (2011), there are stronger correlations between positive relationships and student engagement, than there are between these relationships and academic achievement.

Teachers can work to build relationships and student engagement in a number of ways including, but not limited to:

- Creating a welcome environment in their classrooms
- Developing creative and engaging lessons that allow all students to access the curriculum
- Spending time getting to know their individual students
- Allowing student voice and choice in their classrooms

When students feel comfortable in a teacher's classroom, they are more likely to be engaged in the given content because students know that teachers who take time to build relationships with them will also spend time helping them when they are struggling. Teachers who prioritize relationship-building are more likely to incorporate scaffolding into their lessons, to challenge their students to critically think, as well as to create an environment where questions are welcomed and encouraged. According to a study done by Hansen (2018),

> high expectations and an effective learning environment are closely woven together when developing positive student–teacher relationships. The relationship is strengthened when the learning environment created by the teacher is one that invites inquiry, promotes experimentation (be it right or wrong), and makes connections to deeply learned concepts. (p. 33)

Once students feel comfortable, supported, challenged by their learning environment, and their overall engagement is raised, they may increase their overall academic performance as well. Despite research not showing a strong correlation between positive teacher-student relationships and academic achievement, educators have seen academic growth in students, as well as more willingness to complete work due to these positive relationships.

Roorda et. al (2011) explain in their study how "affective TSRs were associated with both students' school engagement and achievement. In line with the self-determination theory, the smaller associations with achievement seem to suggest that the effect of TSRs on achievement runs partly via engagement" (p. 515). Thus, once students are engaged by a teacher because of their relationships, the students can potentially improve their academic performance.

The reason academic achievement is a main benefit of having a strong teacher-student relationship is because when students feel their teachers care about them and support their academic learning, they are more likely to complete assigned work. Many educators have experienced increases in student effort and work completion as their relationships have grown with these students. Often, when students do not feel support from their teachers, or do not feel comfortable asking for help, they are less likely to complete and submit work for fear of being wrong or failing.

However, if teachers work to build relationships and understand who their students are as individuals, they are more likely to help their students perform better academically. One proven strategy to not only engage the students, but also encourage them to submit work is to relate assignments to their interests. For example, if an educator has a student who is struggling in his or her class or in other classes, but has put in the time to know that this student's interests include cars and working on cars, the teacher could create or tailor assignments for that particular student to incorporate this interest such as changing writing prompts, creating word problems in math about cars, or providing the student choices for assignments and assessments.

If students are given choices, they know their teachers are willing to listen to them and acknowledge their interests outside of the classroom, and may be more likely and willing to complete work for that particular class. When educators give students choices and let them know their interests are valid in their classrooms, they can help the students become more motivated to perform academically. This is proven in the study by Roorda et al. (2011), which concluded that children have basic needs that must be met (the needs for relatedness, competence, and autonomy); once these are met by teachers through various methods, including providing students with choices, their motivation and autonomy in the classroom can increase.

When a teacher puts in the time and effort to create a positive learning environment that fosters positive TSRs, not only can students become more engaged and be more successful in the classroom, but they can also develop skills that will translate outside the classroom, such as self-efficacy and self-advocacy skills. Both research and educators confirm that when students feel supported by their teachers, they are more likely to ask questions, discuss their grades with teachers, seek help, and even seek out challenges because they know the classroom environment supports these actions.

Self-efficacy and self-advocacy are hard skills for students to learn and practice, especially at the high school level where there are multiple pressures to fit in, succeed academically as well as in extracurricular activities, and outside factors. However, when teachers structure their classrooms in a way that lets students explore topics and ideas meaningful to them and where students are encouraged to do their best, and they know they have a teacher behind them who truly cares, it can help develop these skills.

A primary factor in helping students develop self-advocacy and a greater sense of self-efficacy is the way teachers set up their classrooms to support and engage students. In his study, Hansen (2018) interviewed students about the effects of positive TSRs on student learning. One student discussed how his relationship with a teacher had a large impact on how he handled adverse situations in his life. Hansen summed up this interview by saying:

> When teachers have high expectations, even the disciplinary kids work hard in class. High expectations from his teachers was a key contributor to his conquering of adverse situations in his life. He noted that his teachers who had high expectations and provided the support to meet the expectations, made him realize that he could accomplish anything he set his mind to. (2018)

The key here is that the teacher established a positive relationship with the interviewee, created an environment in the classroom that was challenging but also fostered student growth, so the student felt comfortable enough to rise to the challenges he faced and developed a greater confidence in his ability to do so, all the while knowing he would have support along the way.

Teacher–Parent Relationships

Another way to build relationships with students that is less often considered is for teachers to also build relationships with parents. There are many benefits to developing strong and positive relationships with parents, including letting students know teachers care about them, creating open communication lines with parents about all issues, and creating a "team" of support for students. Educators are a resource for parents as their children progress through their educational journeys, and it is part of the job to help the parents understand the academic and non-academic skills teachers want the students to learn in the classroom.

Adams and Christenson (2000) describe it best: "In the best of all possible worlds, the family-school relationship would be based not only on two-way communication, cooperation, and coordination, but also on collaboration" (p. 478). When educators open lines of communication with parents, they can help support their students and reinforce the skills addressed in the classroom.

The main contributing factor to teacher–parent relationships is the trust parents place in their students' teachers, schools, and even the school district. In order to develop and deepen levels of trust, teachers must take an active and early approach to parent communication. When parents have trust in their students' teachers and the school community, it can positively impact their child's educational experience. Research shows that parents' trust in their children's learning teams can positively affect secondary students' credits earned per year, overall GPA, and attendance rates (Adams & Christenson, 2000).

Adams and Christenson (2000) found that the number-one way to increase parent trust is communication between the parents and the teachers. Oftentimes parents only hear from teachers when their child or children are struggling academically, or if they have misbehaved; but when educators communicate with parents only for these reasons, they are not building trusting relationships or developing a team to help the students. It is essential for teachers to open lines of communication with parents early in the school year and to ensure that not all communication is negative. While it is obviously important for teachers to reach out to parents when students are struggling or failing, it is even more important when developing trusting relationships to highlight times when students make progress, succeed in a difficult area, or even do something nice for a peer.

Although building relationships with parents becomes increasingly more difficult at the secondary level because of the large number of students per teacher, it is a vital part of helping students succeed. Research shows there are direct benefits to students' academic success if their parents have trust in their teachers and school community. Communicating and building relationships with parents at any level takes time and effort, but in doing so, teachers are able to demonstrate their commitment to their students' education, their willingness to work with the parents and their students, and to create parent confidence and trust in the teacher's classroom procedures, policies, and curriculum.

WHAT YOU NEED TO KNOW

There are very clear and positive reasons why educators should put in the time and effort to build and maintain positive relationships with their students. When time and effort is invested, teachers will ultimately see less behavior management problems in the classroom, more engaged students, and potentially more completion of work. The biggest key to this is starting before the school year even begins and understanding that building relationships is more than just getting to know students. Furthermore, once the initial relationships are established and the classroom environment is created, teachers must be willing to continually work on these relationships with their students; maintaining and nurturing relationships is even more important than establishing them.

Classroom Culture

A large contributing factor in how students feel in a teacher's classroom, and even their willingness or openness to creating a relationship with a teacher, is how they feel when they enter the classroom for the first time. It is important for teachers to create a welcoming and warm environment that students want to learn and work in. This environment also shouldn't be static, meaning even if teachers think they have created the perfect classroom with the perfect theme, it could still be missing one very important thing: the students' influence.

One great way to build and maintain relationships with students is to continue reflecting *them* in the classroom. Often educators create spaces within their classrooms dedicated to showcasing student work and success. If possible, displaying or showcasing a whole class period of work at a time is most effective, so as to include all students and not leave any out. However, if this is not possible in a particular classroom given space limitations, another great way to showcase student work is cyclically, making sure all students are included at one point in time.

Beyond the physical makeup of a classroom, another approach to developing and maintaining relationships with students is to allow them to take part in choosing classroom norms. At the beginning of the school year it is always tempting for teachers to set the standards and the rules—that is, "these are MY classroom rules"—but if teachers take a more student-centered approach and allow students to suggest some classroom rules and norms, students will not only feel that their voices are heard, but will also recognize that they have ownership in the classroom.

This is also an approach that can help with classroom management; by creating norms as a class, a teacher can always refer back to these when a student misbehaves by saying something like, "I noticed you aren't being respectful to your classmates by talking over them and that is one of our norms, how can we be more respectful going forward?" Many educators have had success with student relationships in this area because students have more connection to the norms they helped to create, and thus are more willing to adhere to them.

Curriculum and Content

One of the most important concepts for teachers to keep in mind when building student relationships is that it "isn't always about the content we teach." There is no denying that many teachers feel overburdened with unrealistic pacing calendars, so deviating from them is a scary thought for any teacher. However, it is important to remember and acknowledge that students won't always remember what they learned in a teacher's classroom, but they will remember how their teachers made them feel. With this in mind, educators should work to find moments in their classrooms where it is appropriate and beneficial to deviate from the lesson plan or scheduled activities to build relationships.

Students are always going to have questions, and many times they will be off topic, or at least tangential to the concepts being covered in class. Although it can be tempting to write off these questions or answer them quickly and refocus the class back to the lesson, these moments can actually be crucial to building and then maintaining relationships with our students. When teachers take the time to acknowledge their students' thoughts and ideas, share stories about themselves, or even admit they don't know the answer to a question and then lead the class through an exercise searching for the answers, they will ultimately create strong bonds with their students. By taking time to do this, students will feel heard and understood. Ultimately, if teachers have created the right environment in their classrooms, and their students enjoy and respect that environment, these types of interactions will not derail a whole lesson and teachers will be able to move students back to the content with ease.

Furthermore, educators should consider their students' interest and learning styles when designing lessons. Although it is not always possible to let student interests dictate what content is being taught, it is possible to incorporate specific activities or types of instruction based on what is known about students and how they learn best. Typically, students learn best with visuals and graphs and through hands-on activity and application, so teachers should keep this in mind while designing lesson plans. The majority of students are *not* auditory learners, which means that lectures and 100% direct instruction is not the most effective way for them to learn.

It is also important—and possible—for teachers to offer student choice, especially regarding assessments. Oftentimes educators create only one assessment for their students at the end of a unit or midway through, the two most common being an essay or a test. However, what most educators know is that these two types of assessments don't always showcase student learning, and alternative assessments may demonstrate a student's understanding of concepts in a better way. Whenever possible, if teachers can provide assessment options for their students, students will engage with the material more and produce better results because they have choice.

Time and Availability

Being available for our students is a crucial part of building relationships with them. Although secondary and elementary teachers see their students for vastly different time periods, each is strapped with time concerns that may limit their availability to help their students. In order for teachers to build strong TSRs, where the students know their teachers support them and are there for them, teachers must be available to their students beyond the given class time. This is not to say teachers need to be available during every free period they have (i.e., before school, in between classes, at lunch, and after school), but teachers should be available to students some of those times.

Being available for students can come in many shapes and sizes, and may look different for each teacher. Sometimes, being available for students might be dictated by what the students need. Some students may be looking for academic help and teachers who are willing to provide them with help. While some students may need help from a teacher whose course they are taking, some students may just be looking for any adult to help them with school work, or at the very least a place they feel comfortable doing work. If a student has a positive relationship with a teacher and needs a place to do school work, they may look toward the teacher's with whom they have the best bond and know will provide the space and opportunity to do work.

Another way teachers may make themselves available for their students is to talk. Educators often wear many hats, and because students spend a majority of their time at schools, one hat that teachers are frequently asked to wear is that of a counselor. If a student has an issue at home or school, they may turn to a trusted teacher for someone to talk to. Although teachers need to keep in mind their job as a mandated reporter, being an ear for students when something is going on in their lives can be a way to build relationships and be available for their students.

Consistency for Parent Contact

Consistency is a key attribute for teachers when building relationships with parents. As mentioned in the previous section, parents often lack trust in their children's teachers and schools, so one way to build that trust and develop relationships is to communicate with parents consistently and often. Research indicates that at the secondary level, teachers communicate with parents less frequently; this may be because they try to handle any situation—good or bad—directly with the student who is almost an adult. At the elementary level, however, communication with parents is necessary for a variety of reasons. If educators develop a consistent routine of communication with students' parents, it will be beneficial for all parties involved.

At the beginning of the school year, teachers can set clear expectations for both parents and students through both the syllabus and back-to-school night, where teachers meet parents for the first time. But after this initial contact, it is just as important to keep communicating with parents, and not just when something has gone wrong. Educators have found success in communicating important information about the classes they teach, including due dates, upcoming large projects, or even opportunities for parents to be involved in their child's learning. This type of communication can allow parents to understand how a teacher's classroom runs and what is expected of the students. When this happens, it can help parents support their students' learning at home and reinforce teacher expectations.

In addition to regular updates and communications about the workings of an educator's classroom, it is important to communicate with parents about individual student progress. While it may seem obvious, it is vitally important to communicate with parents if a student is struggling. However, teachers will not build trust with their students' parents simply by informing them of the difficulties. If an educator communicates with parents when their child is struggling and offers information on how the parents can assist their child, ways the child can improve in the class, and what the teacher is currently doing to help the student, then parents will develop more trust in the teacher and be willing to work with them to help their child.

Early Contact

Early communication with parents can go a long way. If teachers address an issue early, it may not even become an issue. Parents understand that teachers have their students' best interests in mind, and when teachers reach out early and consistently to parents, they are going to be more willing to work with and help teachers reinforce expected behaviors. For example, communicating with a parent about something as simple as a tardy not only communicates the expectations a teacher has for behavior in the classroom, but also expresses a teacher's care and concern for the student.

Communicating the Good

One of the best ways to communicate and build trusting relationships with parents is to communicate with them when their child does something positive in the classroom. Many parents assume that something has gone wrong with their child when they receive a call from the school, but if more teachers reach out to parents about positive things, this stigma could change. Teachers can and should reach out to parents about student progress, when a student excels on a test or project, if a student has done something respectful or kind to/for another student, and many other possibilities.

At the end of the day, educators must remember that parents, students, and the teachers themselves are all important members of the educational team to support student learning. Teachers should keep in mind that they are the experts in their fields and parents don't always know what the expectations are for each classroom, or why teachers might set certain procedures. However, when teachers are willing to communicate with parents early and consistently about classroom expectations, student behavior, and academic progress, then parents will develop the trust in teachers that research shows is lacking.

WHAT YOU CAN DO

First Weeks of School

While it may be tempting for a lot of teachers to start with the syllabus on the first day of school, this approach to the start of the year can be detrimental to building student relationships. Instead, teachers should look to develop relationships with their students and build classroom culture through a variety of methods. During the first few days of school, or even weeks, teachers can look to develop relationships with their students through icebreakers, games, small-group and whole-class activities, writing prompts, and more. This is not to say that establishing classroom policies and procedures is not important; however, students are going to be more willing to follow a teacher's classroom policies if they feel welcomed and part of the classroom from the beginning.

Beyond introductory activities such as icebreakers and "get to know each other" games, teachers can also learn a lot about their students' ideals and expectations for learning by allowing them to develop classroom norms, as discussed above. A more student-centered approach to classroom norms and expectations can help teachers understand their students' expectations for their learning environment and how they learn best.

In research done by Dobransky and Frymier (2004), they discuss power relationships between teachers and students. Traditionally, teachers hold most of the power in a classroom and classrooms are centered around the teacher, but students can also exhibit power through their behaviors. In a classroom where students' needs are not put first, students may exert their power through misbehavior. According to Dobransky and Frymier, "When teachers provide students with choices or allow them to have input into the content covered or other aspects of the class, the teacher is sharing control" (2004, p. 212). A great way to allow students choice while also building relationships with them is to include students in the process of developing the classroom norms and expectations. Furthermore, this can help contribute to the overall classroom culture as all students are more likely to follow and respect the norms because they had a hand in the process.

Follow-Through and Consistency

One of the most important aspects of teaching is creating a classroom environment where the teacher has clear expectations. If a teacher does not follow through with their own rules in the classroom, the students notice and in turn may assume the rule must not be important. A rule or expectation in the classroom that is not enforced should not be a rule or expectation. It will create more problems in the classroom environment if there are rules that exist, but are not enforced.

A teacher who consistently enforces the rules and expectations is an important part of creating a positive learning environment. Furthermore, teachers who create a learning environment with high expectations for their students can also help their students develop self-efficacy, as mentioned above. In his research interviews, Hansen (2018) cites one student's thoughts about teachers setting high expectations: "He noted that his teachers who had high expectations and provided the support to meet the expectations, made him realize that he could accomplish anything he set his mind to" (p. 31). The key here is not just setting high expectations for our students, but also providing them with structure, support, and encouragement to meet those expectations.

In addition to expectations for classroom behavior and for procedures, students are often also looking for curriculum that both engages and challenges them. Most students want to learn and are looking for teachers who engage them with materials that are interesting, but also aren't easy to master. While it might not always seem obvious, students enjoy classrooms where they know teachers will provide rigor and consistently push them to grow as learners. In fact, research found that "Students are keenly aware when teachers genuinely care about their well-being and their education. It is evidenced in the rigor of the instruction, the way they are spoken to, and by understanding the students' circumstances" (Hansen, 2018).

By creating lessons and assessments that are rigorous and engage students, teachers demonstrate care for their students' learning and progress. This idea should be kept in mind when creating lesson plans and developing curriculum throughout the school year. It is not enough to have "one tough lesson"; students need to be consistently challenged to improve, and then supported by their teachers so they can develop self-efficacy and motivation related to their academic work.

Student Feedback and Praise

Positive specific praise is a beneficial tool teachers can use when developing a positive classroom environment and strong TSRs. Positive praise can be used for both student behavior and academic achievement. When teachers reinforce a student's good classroom behavior or specific learning actions, it has a twofold effect. First, when a student exhibits an expected good behavior and teachers reinforce and encourage this behavior, the student is more likely to repeat that same action or behavior (asking a question, turning in an assignment on time, helping another student, etc.). Second, other students will notice the positive attention given to the student for that behavior, which can encourage others in the class to behave in the same way.

It is more beneficial to use other students' positive behaviors as examples than it is to punish or correct a student in front of other students. The tone set in the learning environment is extremely important, and if a key focal point is reinforcing positive behaviors rather than spotlighting negative behaviors, then the classroom becomes a more trusted space to learn, ask questions, and grow as a student. This type of positive reinforcement of behaviors and positive praise can also help strengthen the relationship between the teacher and the students because students understand they will not be called out or singled out for mistakes they make; rather, the teacher will highlight and praise positive behaviors and deal with any negatives in a less public manner.

Beyond behaviors, praise for a student's academic performance is also a crucial component for developing positive relationships between teachers and students. If, and when, teachers acknowledge student successes in the classroom, students learn that their teacher truly cares about them and is willing to support their learning. Furthermore, research suggests that students who receive positive feedback about their academic performance can provide them with motivation to keep learning, and they are likely to become more engaged in the classroom.

Hansen (2018) drew this conclusion from his research: "When a teacher focuses on a child's effort or strategies they have applied to their individual learning, they instill an eagerness in the child to confront new challenges" (p. 32). This kind of feedback and praise can be especially crucial for students who struggle academically. When a teacher provides positive feedback and encouragement to a student who doesn't typically do well academically, it can be the motivating factor for that student to keep working hard and learning.

STUDENT CHECK-INS

Small, simple check-ins with students are a great way to create a positive learning environment in a classroom. Check-ins show children that they are important as students, but also as people. Educators are not only tasked with teaching students the given curriculum, but also helping them grow as individuals in order to become contributing members of society. Checking in with students throughout the period, the week, the unit, or even the quarter about academic and other needs can help students feel comfortable in the given teacher's classroom.

However, it is not enough to simply check in with a student verbally, through writing, or via a Google form; it is what teachers do with the information from the check-ins that matters. For example, if a teacher sends out a weekly survey to their students and one question says "What is one question you still have about the material covered in class this week?" and many students have questions about the same idea, but the teacher never goes back over this idea or revisits it in the next lesson or the next week, then the check-ins aren't a useful tool to build relationships.

However, if a teacher takes time to revisit or re-evaluate how they taught the material students have questions about, and act on it, then the students will know their teacher not only hears their concerns but will also continue to support their learning and look to help them in new ways. This is because, as one student explains, "her former chemistry teacher excelled at communicating with students and in providing help with difficult concepts in class. A student's question in class was always perceived as being important to the teacher, and she took great care in answering the questions without intimating the questions were unwarranted" (Hansen, 2018).

Often, students might feel embarrassed to ask questions or feel stupid for not understanding a concept, but when a teacher creates an atmosphere, through check-ins, in which students know they can ask questions and the teacher will genuinely consider and respond to what they are saying, then students are more likely to respond and engage with that teacher.

Parent Contact

Communicating early and often with parents is a simple way to think of how and when teachers should communicate with parents. While secondary teachers have a larger burden of parent contact given how many students they typically teach, doing something as simple as calling two parents each prep period during the week can be an effective way to tackle parent contact. This same strategy can be used by elementary teachers as well. This is not to say teachers should spend every prep period every day contacting parents, but early on in the school year this is one way to reach out and start establishing those relationships. Even if the parent does not answer or get back to the teacher, the act of reaching out alone shows the parents their child's teacher is interested in their student and willing to communicate to the parents.

Research indicates that parents are less willing to help with school work or reinforce teacher's expectations at home because there is a lack of clear communication between the teachers and the parents (Adams and Christenson, 2000). In our digital age, there is no reason for this lack of communication anymore. If a teacher prefers not to make phone calls to parents, there are other digital ways to communicate that many districts use and pay for, such as email, Google Classroom (where parents can be added to their child's account), Remind, ClassDojo, calendar apps, and many other educational apps that can be used for parent communication. The biggest factor in developing parent–teacher relationships based on trust, in which parents are willing to reinforce teacher expectations in the home, is communication.

One of the easiest ways to start parent communication is at back-to-school night. Most schools hold their back-to-school night during the first few weeks of the school year. This gives teachers the opportunity to not only meet parents who attend in person, but to also make parents aware of the ways teachers will communicate with them and how they can reach out to the teachers. In addition to informing parents how teachers will communicate, this is an opportunity to give parents examples of the types of information that will be regularly communicated to them.

Some important ideas teachers might share with parents are upcoming due dates, important projects or tests, ways parents can help their children study given the current unit, or even ways parents can take part or help in the classroom. It is important to remember parents want to know what is going on in their child's educational experience, and they generally want to support what teachers are doing in the classroom, but are unable to do so unless teachers communicate with them clearly and regularly.

READER TAKEAWAYS

- Building and maintaining positive teacher-student relationships can benefit students' overall academic achievement, increase their engagement in a teacher's classroom, and help them develop meaningful skills such as self-efficacy and self-advocacy.
- Parents often lack trust in teachers and school districts, partially because they lack knowledge of what happens in the classroom and what is expected of their students. Early, consistent, and clear communication with parents will help build trust and foster strong teacher–parent relationships.
- The content taught will not be the main takeaway for students, but if educators provide students with spaces where they feel supported, where they know their voices will be heard, and where they feel comfortable being themselves, then teachers will ultimately provide them with more skills and valuable lessons to use in the world.

REFERENCES

Adams, K., & Christenson, S. (2000). Trust and the family-school relationship: Examination of parent–teacher differences in elementary and secondary grades. *Journal of School Psychology, 38*(5), 477–497. https://doi.org/10.1016/S0022-4405(00)00048-0

Dobransky, N., & Frymier, A. (2004). Developing teacher-student relationships through out of class communication. *Communication Quarterly, 52*(3), 211-223. https://doi.org/10.1080/01463370409370193

Hansen, T. (2018). All because of my teacher: A practical approach to developing positive student–teacher relationships. *Leadership, 47*(4), 30–34.

Roorda, D. L., Koomen, H. M. Y., Split, J. L., & Oort, F. J. (2011). The influence of affective teacher-student relationships on students' school engagement and achievement: A meta-analytic approach. *Review of Educational Research, 81*(4), 493–529. https://doi.org/10.3102/0034654311421793

NINE

Games and Play as a Supportive Part of a Pedagogy of Care

Anthony Avery, Kelly B. Binz, and Melissa S. Williams

A good teacher is like a CANDLE—it consumes itself to LIGHT the way for others.

—Mustafa Kemal Ataturk

EXPECTED LEARNING OUTCOMES

- Understanding the value of games and activities for academic and social and emotional learning (SEL) outcomes
- Build professional confidence through practical application
- Build student communities through intentional and purposeful games
- Create an engaging classroom using specific games and strategies
- Use games and play in the classroom as a pedagogy of care

WHAT WE KNOW

Have you ever made candles from scratch? It is a feat of procedural craftiness that results in a useful and aesthetic object. The candlemaker must gather specific supplies including a double boiler, beeswax, wick, candle holders, and thermometers. The candle holder is measured to gauge the volume of wax, and the maker takes great care in monitoring the thermometer and the candle's resting time. The alchemist also takes great care and satisfaction in mixing fragrances to target discerning consumers.

Such is the passion of the teacher. Much like the candlemaker, educators use the resources available to them and the knowledge of their students to support not only the academic, but also the personal growth of their students. Science, aesthetics, intuition, and the uniqueness of student relationships melt and cool into evolving creations of the human form. Educators strive to give their students purpose and strength of will. They hope to support students in developing grit and resilience, and work to build the empathy and grace of their students.

Creating a classroom environment that supports this development is also a science and an art form. Teachers foster caring environments that build a pedagogy of care. Research continues to support the idea that

> teachers need to understand that caring is an unselfish act and that effective educators continue to demonstrate care even when the care is not reciprocated. Good teaching can be thought of in terms of knowing, loving, and acting for students. The fact that teaching presents hard challenges is not lost especially on those who teach young adolescents, but the effective teacher acknowledges this and yet still continues to love and care for students. (Owusu-Ansah & Kyei-Blankson, 2016, p. 2)

Games and play are an integral part of this methodology. There are four research-based reasons to integrate a sense of play and games into your classroom environment: social and emotional learning (SEL), academic responsibility, brain research, and the joy of teaching. These reflect student needs, critical issues affecting modern schools, and the current drive to increase classroom culture and support students' emotional development.

Social and Emotional Learning

Social and emotional learning (SEL) goals serve the purpose of meeting the nonacademic needs of all students. The education community has recognized the importance of creating opportunities to approach the health and happiness of students' well-being as well as their academics. The National Center on Safe and Supportive Learning Environments (n.d.) states:

Social and emotional learning (SEL) involves the processes through which children and adults acquire and effectively apply the knowledge, attitudes, and skills necessary to understand and manage emotions, set and achieve positive goals, feel and show empathy for others, establish and maintain positive relationships, and make responsible decisions.

Academic Responsibility

The rigor of state and national academic standards is more challenging than ever before. The education system is designed around reading, writing, math, science, history, and technology. Data collection, high-stakes testing, rigor, questioning levels, and technology pressures are forces that define each and every lesson. There is a fear that deviating from the curriculum will negatively impact the pacing calendar and district scope and sequence. Teachers feel this pressure intensely!

Brain Research

In addition, current brain research has identified huge benefits for working and long-term memory when brain breaks are given during thinking and learning. These breaks, while taking minutes away from learning objectives, actually increase the effectiveness and efficiency of a 25- to 40-minute lesson (Hammond, 2015).

The Real Joy of Teaching

Dale Carnegie once said, "People rarely succeed unless they have fun in what they are doing."

The teacher is an emotional and powerful human presence. Teachers must remember that joy is contagious. It sets a tone for positive culture and models that learning can be simply fun. Each educator deserves the permission to be creative, laugh, find joy, and just enjoy facilitating student growth.

One of the most important ingredients of teaching is putting play into the classroom. This takes the form of games, activities, and breaks. Historically, "games" have winners and losers and an inherent sense of competition. In this chapter, games are defined as breaks and activities. The purpose here is to add a valuable aspect of fun that enhances the richness of a pedagogy of care.

Chapter 9

WHAT YOU NEED TO KNOW

Social and Emotional Learning

Recent events have highlighted the need for SEL in classrooms. Now more than ever, students are dealing with stress and anxiety caused by family strife, social pressures, and an inability to maturely process the constant flow of information from an overly connected world. This state of struggle is compounded if the student lives in poverty. The addition of economic hardships comes with feelings of inadequacy, academic challenges, and food insecurity, among other negative circumstances. With so much weighing on the hearts and minds of students, SEL has become a required prerequisite to academic growth.

In order to overcome these obstacles, teachers must create a safe and emotionally comfortable environment where students feel validated enough to take risks and feel fully valued before they can be academically critiqued. The integration of SEL games into the classroom can be the first step. Games of this type are aimed at creating bonds by building relationships through shared experiences. Without a focus on winning or defeating an opponent, SEL games provide engaging experiences where students inadvertently learn more about their classmates, teacher, and themselves.

Before these games can be played successfully, the teacher must create class norms in advance. Students must understand the importance of validating and supporting each other. These norms should be stated and modeled by the teacher from the first day of class. The expectation for all the students in class should be to accept each other and look for ways to praise fellow classmates. This may seem like a fairly simple concept. However, praising and validating one another is a particular set of social skills that students can lack if not modeled in the home.

Students lacking these skills are more likely to negatively react to new and uncomfortable situations. Put-downs and name-calling are common defense mechanisms students use to tear down others in a futile effort to increase their own level of comfort and confidence. Teachers can combat these ingrained behaviors by holding open conversations where students are encouraged to share. The other students are instructed to agree in specific ways.

For example, students can clap or snap their fingers if they agree with the statements made by another student or they want to show support for a classmate. The teacher must clearly state the expectation that the purpose is to share and be positive throughout the day. As students begin to support and reciprocate, the class becomes bonded through the positive talk and actions. This sets the scene for more SEL activities and deeper connections.

All My Neighbors: A Relationship-Building Activity

An example of an SEL game with the sole purpose of creating shared positive experiences is called "All My Neighbors." This game has many rule variations and different ways to play, but is simple at its core. All My Neighbors allows its participants to identify others who have the same likes, preferences, experiences, and viewpoints. In a society where we focus so automatically on our differences, this is a great chance to identify our similarities.

The game is simple and can be played outside using sidewalk chalk. The teacher asks students to stand in a circle and passes out chalk. The students draw a large square around themselves and stand in the middle of it. The teacher will stand in the middle of the group. The teacher is the first "caller." The caller's job is to make a statement starting with the phrase, "All my neighbors who." It is important for the caller to make a statement that is true to themselves.

For example, if the caller loves pizza, then he or she would begin the round by stating, "All my neighbors who love pizza." On the caller's cue, all participants that agree with the statement must leave their spot and find a new square, moving themselves around the circle. The students who disagree will remain in their squares. The caller must also move to one of the empty squares, leaving the last student who is not standing in a square, the new caller. This ensures that one student cannot dominate the game and allows for multiple students to share the calling duties.

As the game progresses, the teacher is a full participant. Remember, the goal of this activity is to build bonds and relationships among the students *and* with the teacher. The teacher's participation is vital to this process because it allows students to see the teacher as not just the authority figure in the classroom, but as a person with his or her own preferences and experiences.

The new caller continues the next round of the game by stating, "All my neighbors who . . ." and finishes the sentence with a personal preference or experience. As the game goes on, all of the participants are engaged in sharing and inadvertently learning about their classmates and teacher.

During an activity like All My Neighbors in which students are encouraged to share openly, there may come a time when the teacher needs to reset the game. Perhaps the students have referenced inappropriate topics, or the topics have become repetitive. Without the need for stern reprimands, which can break the sharing atmosphere, the teacher can reset the game simply by taking a turn as the caller.

This may also be necessary if the teacher is trying to learn more about his or her students and feels the need to push the topics deeper than surface-level preferences. For example, the teacher may take a turn as the caller and state, "All my neighbors whose parents are divorced." This may seem like a topic that should be avoided in casual conversation with

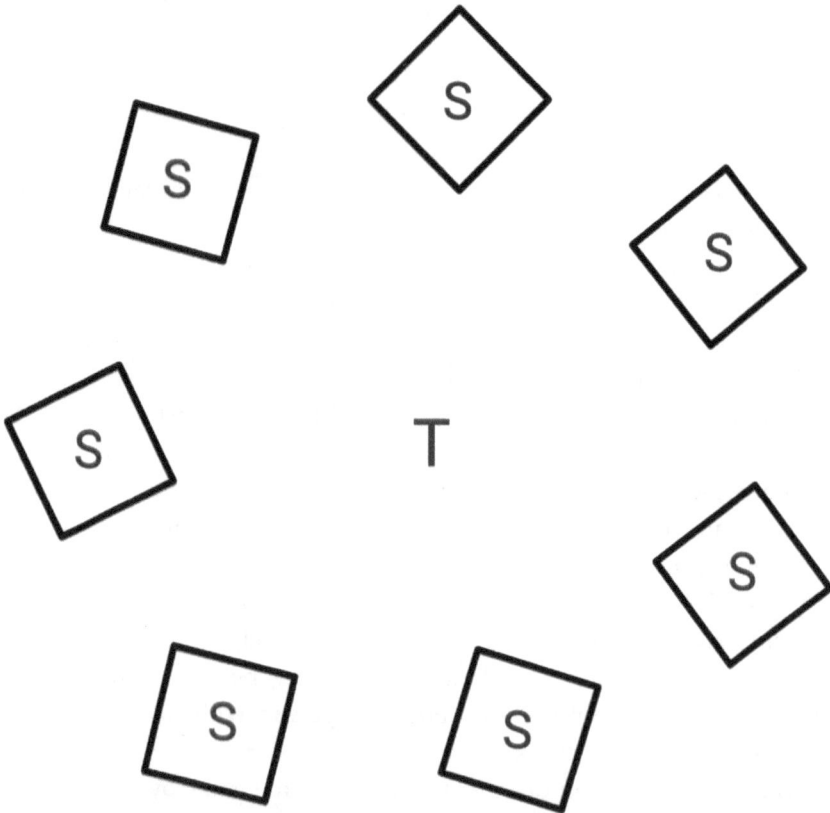

Figure 9.1.   Starting positions.

students. However, this game allows students to share without the fear of follow-up questions or conversations that could become invasive or embarrassing. Students share simply by moving to a new circle, in some cases unaware that they have shared a personal situation they may not have felt comfortable divulging otherwise.

It is important for the teacher to take mental notes of these preferences and experiences. This information should serve as a roadmap for the teacher to know which boundaries not to cross, which students may be sensitive to certain topics, who shares readily, and who is reluctant to share. These activities can allow the teacher to show a level of respect for a student's situations outside of class. This modeled reverence by the teacher will add to the class expectation of positive support of all.

Where to go from here? Remember, the ultimate goal of a teacher is to support the emotional well-being of the students and to help the students reach academic success. With the knowledge learned from the SEL game, the teacher can design learning experiences that cater to individual students on a deeper level. Perhaps the teacher will start a journal conversation in which the student writes a journal entry and the teacher responds specifically to that student in their journal. Maybe the teacher will choose specific reading materials for the entire class with a preference toward sports or arts. The teacher can also develop incentives or earned experiences tailored to a specific group of students.

Academic Responsibility

Teachers have the goal of teaching students to deepen their understanding of an academic objective. They "hook" students into a lesson and then begin the direct instruction. As modeling and guided practice give way to independent practice, a game can serve many functions. These include gathering formative data, providing repetition, increasing engagement through listening, speaking, reading, and writing, and providing strategies for students to move information from working to long-term memory.

Teachers strive to create rich "tier 1" instruction. This ensures that mastery is attainable, students are engaged, and learning objectives are met. These lessons grab students' attention, build schema, execute a design that matches the curriculum objective, and account for modification and accommodations that scaffold up and down from the expected grade level. Summative assessments, in various forms, provide valuable data, but play as a formative assessment can be powerful. Let's consider that the time spent planning the instruction is much greater than the actual time spent delivering instruction. Teachers may feel like there's simply no more room for another aspect of the lesson plan. However, consider the critical value of intentional use of games as a part of a pedagogy of care in the classroom.

"By inclusion of frequent processing time, brain-breaks, and energizers, a good teacher keeps the energy in the room high and minds focused" (Kagan & Kagan, 2009). The goal of every lesson is for 100% of learners to demonstrate active engagement with instruction. This engagement may appear as evidence of listening through facial expressions, head nods, and/or eye contact; verbalization of comments or questions; and written notes or drawings. The teacher's responsibility is to monitor engagement and learning. Games are a perfect way to meet this requirement.

Games can be intentionally selected to increase kinesthetic association to skills. Several academic games lend themselves to movement and discourse. Physical activity increases brain connections and endorphins. Both side effects increase active learning.

Games and play provide repetition and increase long-term memory. Rich classrooms activate students before, during, and after instruction. The repetition of visuals, purposeful peer talk, and note-taking or doodling are effective ways to influence human memory. Playing a game touches on the emotional connections, and on visual and verbal repetition.

When skills are paired with games and connected to prior experiences, memory is increased. In one study, vocabulary learning was increased by 20% when students were exercising (Terada, 2018). When skills are paired with games and connected to prior experiences, learning is richer. Harry Wong, in his 1998 book, *The First Days of School: How to Be an Effective Teacher*, identifies repetition as an integral step toward establishing classroom routines. Students are less likely to forget the skills that make them smile and play.

There is an innate problem-solving aspect to games. Most creative learning games partner students and require verbalization of a process or justification of an answer. Turn-taking, speaking, listening, learning nonverbal cues, encouragement, and solving conflicts are all positive outcomes beyond the actual academic skill objective.

Finally, play and games lay the foundation for students to make deeper connections to ideas and attain a depth of knowledge greater than basic understanding. Several curricula, including Common Core State Standards and Texas Assessment of Knowledge and Skills, delineate verbiage that goes much deeper than remembering facts and explaining a sequence. A caring classroom culture supports students through these depths. Students are not left without strategies to find mastery and success. Teachers who include opportunities for students to justify their answers, make connections, and synthesize information use games to their advantage.

Dance It, Chance It: An Academic Game

One energizing game listed on the website Lead4ward.com offers a deep dive into the depths of knowledge. Called, "Dance It, Chance It," the game is really an injection of play and music into guided practice. It incorporates songs, dance, peer conversation, turn-taking, and justification of answers.

To play, access the Lead4ward.com website to find a premade template of several presentation slides. Each can be edited to include questions and answers corresponding to a current lesson.

The first slide encourages students to dance to a tune. When the music stops, students pair up. The next slide instructs students to read a question-and-answer choice. Player 1 takes a chance to answer and justify the correct answer. Player 2 takes a chance and selects an answer choice that may trick someone. Player 2 also explains why that answer choice is incorrect. The teacher pauses the class to take responses and clarify and verify understanding. Then, the dancing continues.

The investment of planning for play and games is not fruitless! The pedagogy of care is increased by the intentionality of the educators who consider the purpose of games to be a support for academics.

Brain Breaks

Brains are powerful, yet easily tired. On average, brains can attend to learning specific skills for 12- to 20-minute chunks depending on various factors (Schmidt-Kassow et al., 2013). They are most efficient when challenged, then given time to relax and process.

Why Take Brain Breaks?

Teachers aim to get the most out of the constraints of their given "blocks" of time. Classrooms that incorporate intentional and preplanned brain breaks lay the foundation for a less stressful learning environment and ensure increased mastery of skills.

There is an inclination to feel as though planning time to "break" subtracts from the limited, precious time scheduled for the class. It seems counterintuitive to give time to something else, but research has proven the opposite. Taking time to pause the brain will allow students to temporarily move away from the overload of academic learning and allow the mind to refresh for new learning. It is imperative to understand that sometimes we need to slow down in order for optimal learning and attention to occur.

The beauty of brain breaks is that they basically require zero to minimal prep time, but are ultimately alluring and possible. Brain breaks can be intentionally preplanned but are also effective when they are spontaneous. These are meant to be short and provide activity that boosts the flow of oxygen to the brain. The purpose of brain breaks is to not disrupt the flow of learning, but to rejuvenate the brain through stretching, moving around the room, singing, and dancing to restore student focus.

The teacher should examine the daily lesson plan and think about placing breaks that are suitable for students based on age and classroom culture. Brain breaks can vary from calming to active. When deciding on which form of brain break to incorporate into the daily schedule, the teacher might want to consider the intensity of the lesson delivered prior to implementing a brain break.

Think in terms of opposites. For example, if the lesson was engaging and required an intense level of brain activity and movement, the teacher should contemplate using a calming brain break. This is a prime opportunity to relax student minds and bodies. These activities create a calming mechanism to allow students to bring their energy level down a bit and to rejuvenate the brain so that optimal learning may occur.

Deep Breathing: Power and Refuel the Brain

One example of a calming brain-break strategy is guided deep breathing. In this activity, the teacher sets the expectation that students will find a personal place in the room and remain quiet and respectful for the next three minutes. Students should be in a relaxed position and close their eyes. The teacher guides students to take an exaggerated breath for three seconds, hold for two seconds, and exhale for four seconds. Students can imagine exhaling stress and worry through this technique. The goal of consistent implementation and practice is for students to become self-aware and begin to self-regulate.

On the other hand, some instructional lesson cycles incorporate a "sit and get" style. This may include note-taking, watching a video, or listening. This type of learning can be exhausting to the brain. Brain breaks of an active nature are much more beneficial in these situations. Active brain breaks stimulate the brain and increase a students' physical activity. The goal is for students to return to the task more focused and for the brain to feel re-energized.

30-Second Dance Break: Energize the Brain

One example of an active brain-break strategy is a "30-Second Dance Break." Before class begins, the teacher should collect music suggestions from the students. The teacher should carefully preview song choices and lyrics, and can create a weekly playlist of songs. Brain breaks need to be taught in order for them to be effective. After 12 to 20 minutes of instruction, the teacher announces a 30-second dance break. Students are allowed to dance appropriately near their desks until the music stops. The teacher should engage with and enjoy the music, too. When the music stops, students return to their seats and to a learning position to continue the lesson.

When students know the expectations and the purpose of brain breaks, these activities are most effective. These small moments in a classroom will ease frustration and exhaustion and refresh the brain for new learning experiences.

WHAT YOU CAN DO

Tables 9.1, 9.2, and 9.3 constitute a quick reference guide for classroom teachers. This list of resources is by no means exhaustive, but offers several low- or no-prep games and activities. Integrating a few of these into lesson plans will marry the science of teaching and the art of learning.

Table 9.1. Brain-Break Activities

Activity	Type	Resource	Need To Know
Minute to Win It	Active	YouTube search	• Minute to Win It games often require supplies and set-up time. • Students will need time to practice the games and take turns. It may help the teacher to create one activity that can be played repeatedly. • Because these games can be time-consuming, the teacher should account for that extra time in weekly class planning.
GoNoodle	Active	gonoodle.com	• GoNoodle is a website that offers songs and videos that range from educational to just for fun. • After signing up for an account, the teacher can use GoNoodle for a quick and easy dance break. • The integration of the educational GoNoodle videos can add a kinesthetic element that could be repeated during a lesson.
Gallery Walk	Active	https://www.edutopia.org/blog/enliven-class-discussion-with-gallery-walks-rebecca-alber	• A gallery walk can be used in a variety of ways in a classroom. The teacher or the students post work, pictures, and questions around the room. • Then the students work in small groups to rotate around the room. • At each stop the group responds to questions, critiques/gives feedback on the work of others, or creates something based on a prompt. • For a brain break, the teacher could post ideas or prompts for drawing, and the students could respond by drawing on sticky notes.
Head's Up Seven Up	Active	YouTube search	• Heads Up Seven Up can be a time-consuming game to play. An important tip for the teacher is to set a number of rounds from the beginning. This will limit the disruption to the schedule. • The game is simple! The teacher chooses seven students to tag others during the round. • The teacher instructs the other students to put their heads down, close their eyes and put one thumb up.

Activity	Type	Resource	Need To Know
			• The seven taggers then quietly move around the room and tap the thumb of one person. • When all seven taggers have chosen one person by tapping their thumbs, the teacher calls "heads up seven up." • The seven chosen students stand up and take turns trying to figure out who tagged them through the process of elimination.
Charades	Active	Google search	• Charades is a classic game that is quick and requires no setup. • This game can also be played in small groups, which may be an efficient way to minimize the class schedule disruption. • The directions are simple! A student is chosen to act out a word or phrase without saying any words. • The other students try to guess the word or phrase. • This can be a great way to teach a sensory language.
TikTok Dance	Active	tiktok.com YouTube search	• TikTok is an app for sharing short videos of all types. One of the most popular uses of the TikTok app is dance videos. • The teacher can find these dance videos on the TikTok app or on YouTube as a compilation. • It is important for the teacher to preview the video before showing it to the class. • When the teacher feels the class needs an active break, he or she can play the video and allow the students to dance. • These TikTok videos could even be sent to the students in advance, allowing students to practice. This would also allow students to be creative and make up their own dances to show the class.
Quick Draw	Calming	quickdraw.with google.com/	• Doodling, or quick drawing activities, can be a calming addition to a classroom. • The teacher needs to have scrap or construction paper and pencils readily available to make this break quick.

Activity	Type	Resource	Need To Know
			• The teacher should set a timer and explain to the students the expectations of transitioning back to work after the designated time. • Quick Draw is a timed-guided online activity that asks users to quickly draw common objects. The site then allows users to compare drawings to similar drawings by other users.
Stretching	Calming	gonoodle.com	• GoNoodle offers many quick stretching videos for ease of use. • Including stretching into a daily classroom routine can set the tone for a relaxed and focused learning environment. • Stretching can be used at the beginning of class to help students reframe their day. • The teacher should set a timer and explain to the students the expectations for transitioning back to work after the designated time.
Meditation	Calming	gonoodle.com	• GoNoodle offers many quick meditation videos for ease of use. • Including meditation into a daily classroom routine can set the tone for a relaxed and focused learning environment. • Meditation can be used at the beginning of class to help students reframe their day. • The teacher should set a timer and explain to the students the expectations of transitioning back to work after the designated time.
Music	Calming	YouTube search, music streaming	• Music can be integrated in a classroom in many ways. • The teacher may choose to use classical music to set a calm and focused classroom. • The teacher may choose to use a fast-tempo song for competitions or time efforts.
Sculpting Foil or Play-Doh	Calming		• Shape and save thematic visuals to connect to literature, vocabulary, or historical figures. • Foil and Play-Doh can also be used for a timed relaxation activity.

Activity	Type	Resource	Need To Know
Brain-Break Videos	Calming	https://teachingwithamountainview.com/brain-break-videos-that-your-kids-will/	• The resource listed for this activity offers a variety of fun videos for students to watch. • The videos are meant for quick nonacademic break times.

Table 9.2. Academic Activities

Activity	Type	Resource	Need to Know
Instructional Strategies Playlists	Academic	https://lead4ward.com/playlists/	• Navigate to the Instructional Strategies playlist • There is also a new Virtual Instructional Strategies playlist
Brain Teasers	Academic		• Ask students to draw connections between classic art and subject matter • Challenge students to create their own brain teasers for the class
Sequence Cards	Academic	ThinkingMaps.com	Apply across subject areas: • History timelines • Science procedures • Narrative retelling • Math algorithms
Would You Rather . . . (Simple/complex)	Academic	There are many resources online. Begin with non-academic question stems, then continue with opinions about the subject matter. Extend to ask students to support their answers.	• Allows students to process opinions and find commonalities between their thinking and the thinking of others in their classroom
Picture This . . .	Academic		• A game like the popular board game Pictionary • Ask students to draw associations and group them by commonality or differences

Activity	Type	Resource	Need to Know
Character Pantomime	Academic		• Increases character traits and vocabulary • Can impact empathy • Increases depth when paired with dialogue or quotes from text
Readers' Theater	Academic	Scholastic: https://www.scholastic.com/librarians/programs/rt_resources.htm Teachers Pay Teachers: https://www.teacherspayteachers.com/	• Extends the thinking of gifted and talented students • Students can stay socially distant • Simple costumes can add to the fun • Visuals, props, backdrops can engage all learners
Music/Song Writing	Academic		• Taking the most important details of a lesson and setting them to music has powerful effects on memory • Increases understanding of literary elements, especially in poetry

Table 9.3. Social and Emotional Learning Activities

Activity	Type	Resource	Need to Know
• 60-Second Relate Break • 90-Second Spark • Treatment Agreement • 2-Minute Connection • Pulse Meter • Get To Know You Circles	SEL	National Educators for Restorative Practices: https://nedrp.com/six-tools-relational-restorative-practices/	National Educators for Restorative Practices offers free articles, instructions, and videos related to six restorative practices that can be easily integrated into any classroom.
Team-Building Games	Team-building	We Are Teachers: https://www.weareteachers.com/team-building-games-and-activities/	We Are Teachers offers a variety of team-building games, including directions.

READER TAKEAWAYS

- Games and activities are valuable for both academic and social and emotional learning.

- Educators' professional confidence in practical application of games and play will be empowered and boosted.
- Classroom communities are strengthened through games and play.
- Specific games and strategies create engaging and rich classrooms.
- Games, play, and humor support a pedagogy of care in the classroom.

REFERENCES

Hammond, Z. (2015). *Culturally responsive teaching and the brain: Promoting authentic engagement and rigor among culturally and linguistically diverse students.* Corwin.

Kagan, M., & Kagan, S. (2009). *Kagan cooperative learning.* Kagan.

Lead4ward. (2020, May). Instructional strategies playlists for teachers. https://lead4ward.com/docs/instructional_strategies/playlist_may_2020_21.pdf

National Center on Safe and Supportive Learning Environments. (n.d.) *Social emotional learning.* Retrieved 16 December 16, 2020, from https://safesupportivelearning.ed.gov/hot-topics/social-emotional-learning

Owusu-Ansah, A., & Kyei-Blankson, L. (2016). Going back to the basics: Demonstrating care, connectedness, and a pedagogy of relationship in education. *World Journal of Education, 6*(3), 1–9. doi:10.5430/wje.v6n3p1

Schmidt-Kassow, M., Deusser, M., Thiel, C., Otterbein, S., Montag, C., & Reuter, M., et al. (2013). Physical exercise during encoding improves vocabulary learning in young female adults: A neuroendocrinological study. *Plos ONE, 8*(5), e64172. doi: 10.1371/journal.pone.0064172

Terada, Y. (2018). *Research-tested benefits of breaks.* Edutopia. https://www.edutopia.org/article/research-tested-benefits-breaks

Wong, H. (1998). *The first days of school.* Harry K. Wong Publications.

TEN

Making Space for Mindfulness

Samantha Houston-Crook

> Between stimulus and response, there is a space. In that space is our power to choose our response. In that response lies our growth and our freedom.
>
> —Viktor Frankl

EXPECTED LEARNING OUTCOMES

- Readers will be able to understand the importance of mindfulness and its impact on executive function in children and adolescents.
- Readers will be able to guide themselves and others through mindfulness exercises that can be implemented in the classroom.

WHAT I KNOW

In today's society an individual may have a to-do list of numerous items, including family obligations and career obligations. In this fast-paced world, oftentimes an individual may forget to "check in" on themselves. The same can go for students. Students and teachers both have so much on their plates daily that they will eventually burn out and become too stressed, anxious, or depressed to manage the complexities of life.

It is very common for children and teenagers to have fears and worries regarding different aspects of their lives, or even to feel sad or lonely.

However, when those feelings are not addressed, they have the potential to manifest into devastating socio-emotional issues.

Anxiety in children and teenagers may interfere with school, home, and play activities. While some individuals may display anxiety as fear or worry, others may become irritable or angry, have trouble sleeping, experience fatigue, headaches, or stomachaches. Different types of anxiety disorders include:

- Being afraid when parents are away (separation anxiety)
- Having extreme fears about specific things or situations (phobias)
- Being afraid of school, groups, or other places where there are people (social anxiety)
- Being worried about the future or bad things happening (general anxiety)
- Exhibiting repeated episodes of sudden, unexpected, intense fear along with distressing physical symptoms such as pounding heart, trouble breathing, or shaky/sweaty hands (panic disorder) (American Psychiatric Association, 2013)

Additionally, depression in children and teens is very different than the occasional sad or hopeless feeling that people may experience. When children feel sad or uninterested in activities that they previously enjoyed, or feel hopeless in situations that they are able to change, then they may be dealing with symptoms of depression. Other notable behaviors that point to a depressive disorder include:

- Feelings of sadness, hopelessness, or irritability for a majority of the time
- Not wanting to engage in fun activities that were previously enjoyed
- Changes in eating patterns (eating a lot more or a lot less than usual)
- Changes in sleeping patterns (sleeping a lot more or a lot less than normal)
- Changes in energy (feeling fatigued, sluggish, tense, or restless)
- Poor concentration
- Feelings of worthlessness, uselessness, or unnecessary guilt
- Self-injurious or self-destructive behavior (American Psychiatric Association, 2013)

The goal for educators is to allow students to learn in the least restrictive environment possible. The classroom must be a comfortable, safe, and relaxed setting. Teachers not only provide students with the necessary tools to learn, but the skills to eventually become productive adults in society. This can happen by incorporating mindfulness into the classroom environment daily.

Mindfulness is often confused with meditation. While meditation is a great skill to practice in mindfulness, it is not the only aspect of mindfulness. Through mindfulness, people can become more aware of what is going on around them. People experience mindfulness in unexpected ways, whether noticing the crisp fall air while walking on a trail or connecting with another individual on a level that makes the world stand still. However mindfulness happens, the feeling of being present is always available, especially when it comes to times of difficulty or pressure.

Through the work of Jon Kabat-Zinn, stress reduction through mindfulness practice takes its roots from Buddhist and Hindu teachings of *sati* or "mindfulness" as a technique to support individuals struggling with various mental health illnesses (Kabat-Zinn & Hanh, 2013). Through Kabat-Zinn's work, the practice of Mindfulness-Based Stress Reduction was formed in order to treat pain, anxiety, and stress. It has consistently been shown to lower stress levels, reduce the risk of anxiety and depression, and help individuals better cope with rejection or social isolation (Goldin & Gross, 2010). Mindfulness has proven to be a viable practice to incorporate into the classroom in order to provide a more enriching experience for all students.

Mindfulness stresses that users must align themselves in the present, taking control over their bodies and creating a sense of stillness in their bodies and minds. By being rooted in the present, a person is able to develop attentional control. For children who suffer from anxiety, this process allows them to find a place where the worry and fear can be calmed and they know that what they are worrying about will happen later; mindfulness draws them back into the present moment, allowing for more learning opportunities.

In the same way, mindfulness in the classroom can be beneficial for children who suffer from other forms of psycho-socio-emotional trouble such as attention deficit/hyperactivity disorder or trauma, or for children on the autism spectrum in order to create a sense of calm within their school day. Not only does mindfulness allow students to feel in control of their emotions, but it also grants them the autonomy to know that they can create the calmness themselves.

WHAT YOU NEED TO KNOW

The ultimate goal of mindfulness is to teach the students how to self-regulate and create a sense of self-awareness. Mindfulness can begin at any age. Children have opportunities all around them to develop the skills necessary for self-regulation and executive function. These skills are vital for emotional and cognitive development and learning, which create a wide range of positive behaviors that open up the child to more healthy choices.

The brain functions in three different ways: working memory, mental flexibility, and self-control. The working memory is responsible for governing the ability to retain and manipulate pieces of information over short periods of time. Mental flexibility helps to sustain or shift the individual's attention to different demands and apply the necessary rules in these different settings. Self-control enables the individual to set priorities and resist impulsive actions or responses. When a child learns and applies the necessary executive function skills, the brain is able to operate more cohesively.

Humans are not born with these executive functioning skills and have to work to develop them in order to become more well-rounded adults. Children who come from environments where the conditions they need from their relationships with adults are not met (e.g., toxic stress, or exposure to neglect, abuse, or violence) may be subject to delays or impairment in their executive functioning. Growth-promoting environments such as classrooms provide a space for children to practice these skills no matter what type of home the child comes from. By helping students establish routines, modeling social behavior, and creating supportive and reliable relationships, school staff also can help shape how a child self-regulates through mindfulness.

The association between mindfulness in the form of meditation and executive functioning has been observed by numerous neuroscientists. The idea that short-term meditation practice improves executive functioning was tested by Fan and colleagues (2014). Researchers found that after five days of integrative body-mind training or relaxation training, the executive functioning increased and participants showed enhanced moods, attention, and self-regulation due to the interaction between the central (brain) and autonomic (body) systems (Fan et al., 2014).

The idea that meditation increases executive functioning was further explained by Teper and Inzlicht (2013), who reported that even novice meditators experienced a period of emotional acceptance that both improved executive functioning and helped regulate emotions.

Pulling this all together—mindfulness plays a huge role within the classroom. The correlation between executive functioning and academic achievement is high, indicating that children are better equipped to sit still, pay attention, follow rules, control impulses, wait their turn, and be flexible to new ideas and perspectives when mindfulness is utilized; thus, allowing the child to gain confidence, retain more knowledge, and have more positive social interactions with peers and teaching staff.

Socioeconomically disadvantaged children need to implement mindfulness skills as part of their executive functioning training. Children from lower socioeconomic-status communities have been shown to have higher levels of stress hormones and lower levels of executive functioning skills, which pose a risk to healthy neurocognitive development and adaption (Zelazo et al., 2018). Teaching children to both pause and reflect before responding—in other words, by encouraging more mindful moments—allows these children to be more intentional in their behavior and to use more problem-solving skills or reflection. This, in turn, may allow for more improvement in emotional regulation that can reduce social anxiety, depression, and rumination on negative events.

For children, mindfulness training should be designed as a way to foster awareness of the individual internal states. An example of this is teaching the child to describe how different parts of their bodies feel from head to toe. Play-based education, guided by a facilitator, utilizes games like "Simon Says" or "Head–Shoulders–Knees–Toes" to get children to identify with the feelings in their bodies, or employs a hula hoop to create attention "zones" around their bodies. Another activity might incorporate placing a stuffed animal on children's abdomens to aid in breathing as they lie on the ground. The children can watch the stuffed animal go up and down while they breath, thus regulating their breathing.

School-based mindfulness can be applied from kindergarten through grade 12. In 2015, a study was conducted on 99 fourth and fifth graders in public school settings. One group received mindfulness training, while the other group did not receive the training. After all of the measures were analyzed (behavioral assessment, cortisol levels, feedback from peers, and academic scores), the students were found to show dramatic differences. Of the individuals who were trained in school-based mindfulness, 24% had more positive social behaviors, while 20% were reported as being less aggressive. The mindfulness group surpassed the control group in areas related to attention, memory, emotional regulation, stress levels, mindfulness, empathy, and optimism (Schonert-Reichl et al., 2015).

WHAT YOU CAN DO

Teachers are essential for teaching children impulse control and awareness. Before a teacher implements mindfulness techniques in the classroom, it is important for them to either practice or have sufficient understanding of mindfulness. Teachers are constantly under stress and pulled in different directions. Having a teacher or instructor who practices mindfulness in daily life gives the students a role model for how to have appropriate self-awareness and regulation.

The following are examples of activities that can be used to incorporate mindfulness into the classroom.

Body Scan Meditation

This particular intervention is a powerful tool in bringing awareness of locations in the body that may be dysregulated or feel as if there is a lack of control. It encompasses a systemic evaluation of the body using the mind, bringing attention to various regions. Focus begins from the toes of the feet then moving to the entirety of the foot—the sole, heel, top of the foot—then up the legs, ankles, shin, calf, and so on.

Body scan meditation results in a greater awareness of each point of the body. The idea of the body scan allows for full attention to be brought to real-time experiences, or the present moment, and to explore both the pleasant and unpleasant sensations that the individual may be feeling in their bodies. This exercise is best done lying down in a quiet space with the eyes closed. Attention is first brought to the breath and wherever there is touch or pressure on the seat or floor. Sensations to look for include buzzing, tingling, pressure, tightness, or temperature, or maybe nothing at all. Emotional reactions that may be noticed during the body scan can range from impatience, release, sadness, frustration, enjoyment, and boredom, as well as others. Thoughts that shift within the brain can be planning, wishing, or hoping, reviewing the past or imagining the future, circular thinking, or judging the current experience.

When the mind wanders, it is common and acceptable to notice one's drift from awareness and gently bring the mind back toward the sensations within the body. This gentle shift of attention from and back to the place of focus during this exercise allows for new pathways to be created within the brain.

To implement guided body scan for students:

1. Have the students lie on the floor with their eyes closed or looking at the ceiling.
2. Encourage the students to pay attention to their feet for 5–10 seconds. Questions to ask them to contemplate might include: "How does this body part feel?" "Is it warm or cold?" "Does it feel tight or relaxed?" "Is all or part of this body part touching the floor?"
3. Move their attention to the toes, then ankles, then calves and knees, continuing with each body part until they reach the head.
4. When you guide the student to bring awareness to their chest, allow them time to recognize the rise and fall of their chest as they take long, deep breaths.
5. After you have reached the students' heads, allow them a few moments to rescan their body and shake out any tightness or discomfort that they may have felt.

Once a body scan is completed, students will be more relaxed, making this the perfect activity to use after recess or a physical education class when their energy is high in order to get their minds focused.

Breathing Hands

When students feel dysregulated, they may feel they have no control of their breathing. This may occur if they fall on the playground, become too overwhelmed with an assignment, or are even just experiencing a tough day. Breathing hands is a wonderful exercise to open the student toward the awareness that by regulating their breathing, they are able to accomplish their desired goal.

1. Have students spread a hand out like a star.
2. Using the index finger on the other hand, help students trace the outline of their star hand. This requires you to mime the same breathing technique.
3. Inhale as the finger moves to the top of the thumb.
4. Exhale as the finger moves down between the thumb and first finger.
5. Take another inhalation as the finger slowly moves to the top of the first finger.
6. Exhale as the finger moves down between the first and second finger.
7. This process is repeated until five slow, deep breaths are completed.

This is a great activity for the students to do both by themselves and with an adult. Using the visual nature of tracing the hand, the student is able to become more mindful of the lengths of their breaths, drawing them away from distressing thoughts or feelings.

Mindful Sounds

This activity is a wonderful activity for bringing attention to a certain object, making students more mindful of how they experience the noise. This can be done using a meditation cymbal or a singing bowl, or through a phone meditation app that offers these recorded sounds.

1. Begin with three deep breaths.
2. Give students these instructions before ringing the bell:
   - "When I ring the bell, concentrate on the sound that you hear. Pay attention to whether the sound is louder in one ear or the other."
   - "Keep your eyes closed until the sound is completely gone and you can no longer hear it. If you find that your mind is wondering, bring the attention back to the sound of the bell."
   - "After you open your eyes, remain silent until my voice is heard again."
3. The activity is complete when the sound has completely disappeared.

Glitter Bottle

A sensory bottle is a great resource to have in the classroom, especially when students exhibit a variety of disruptive behaviors within the classroom. Glitter jars or "calm down jars" assist students (and adults) with self-regulation, special needs, big emotions, anxiety or stress, boredom relief, or even as a timer.

A glitter jar can be made using the following materials:

- clean plastic bottle or mason jar
- hot water
- mixing bowl
- whisk
- liquid watercolor or food coloring
- clear liquid hand soap
- glitter (any glitter will work except glitter glue).

Combine all ingredients in a mixing bowl, whisk vigorously, then pour into the bottle right away. Put the lid on and shake the bottle to make sure the jar is working. If it is, take the lid off to allow the water to come back to room temperature. After the mixture is cooled, secure the lid on the jar with hot glue or super glue.

The student watches the glitter jar as the displaced glitter swirls to the bottom of the jar. The visual stimulation allows the individual time to calm down, regain control, and regulate their emotions. Glitter jars can be used to teach children and adolescents abut feelings, anger management, and mindfulness.

Five Senses Activity

The five senses activity works best in helping older students calm their bodies and become more mindful of the present. When the mind is busy, it is hard to be aware of what is going on in the present moment and the surroundings. Teaching students the Five senses activity allows them to reorientate themselves to what is going on around them. This is also a great activity to have displayed in the classroom on a poster or on a whiteboard so that the students can reference it during stressful or anxiety-provoking moments during class. Encourage the student to notice:

- Five things they can see
- Four things they can touch

- Three things they can hear
- Two things they can smell
- One thing they can taste

Timer Breaths

Timer breaths is an easy activity to incorporate into daily class time and can be used as a transition tool within the class day. This particular activity allows children to learn to calm themselves down, or simply provide a few moments for silence and stillness.

The teacher will begin by setting a timer for an age-appropriate length; for example, preschool- and kindergarten-age students should not have more than 2 minutes on the timer, while sixth grade students can work up to 10 minutes at a time for timer breaths.

Instruct the students to sit cross-legged on the floor, sit on a chair, or go outside and sit on the grass. Have the students breath in and out deeply, with no talking, until the timer goes off. Remind students to pay close attention to any sounds that they may hear around them or any sensations in their body. By incorporating mindful breaths at fixed times during the class day, the student will recognize that they have the power to calm their bodies and may utilize these mindful breaths at other times during their day.

Worry Bubbles

Anxiety is a common feeling among school age children and adolescents. An activity to give students who may feel like their worry and anxiety is overflowing is the worry bubbles. This activity is best suited for younger children and works well with preschool to second grade students in recognizing what worry is and how to deal with it.

Purchase or make a jar of bubbles. Ask the student to think about a worry that bothers them. Instruct them to blow a bubble and imagine filling it with their worries. Now that worry is trapped inside the bubble and no longer in their body. Watch as the bubble floats away or pops. Let the student know that this worry can no longer bother them and encourage them to continue blowing bubbles until all their worries have floated away.

Morning Mantras

Words are influential to children and adolescents. They can tear a person down or build them up. By telling a child that they are bad, they will continue to be bad. However, by telling a child that they are good, they will continue to strive for that goodness. It is important to always tell a student "good job," as they will hold onto that message and continue to work toward positive messages.

Instead of using put-down language such as "do not do that" or "stop being naughty," a child will benefit from language that is both positive and provides guidance. This includes words such as "I asked you to do (x), but you did (y). Let's brainstorm how you could have followed the teacher's directions to do what you were asked." This technique both redirects the student toward the intended action while also letting them know that their action was not what was expected.

In the same fashion, the way that children speak to themselves influences how they respond to the external stimuli around them. If a child has consistent negative self-talk such as "I am not worthy" or "I cannot do this activity good enough," that child will continue toward that negative mindset, ruining their day and inhibiting any learning moments that can arise.

Instead, start the class day with morning mantras. There is no better way to start the day then reminding students that they are loved, and everything is okay. Instruct the students to sit tall in their chairs and close their eyes. Have them take 10 long, deep breaths in order to center themselves in the present, and instruct them to repeat after you. Repeat together phrases such as, "I am safe and loved," "I am happy and healthy," "I will be kind today," "I am blessed," "I am smart," "I believe in myself," "I am a good kid," "I will try my best," and "I choose to be happy." Phrases like these allows the student to start their day with positivity. The more they repeat these phrases, the more they consolidate in their minds as true. Encouraging this positive self-talk requires both the student and the teacher to practice daily. Students are like sponges, so if the teacher or parent demonstrates negative self-talk, the student will also mimic that type of behavior.

STOP or RAIN

When a student is feeling frustrated, upset, or disconnected from the present, remind them to use the acronym STOP:

- **Stop:** Take a brief pause, no matter what is being done.
- **Take a breath:** Feel the sensation of the body breathing, bringing awareness back to the present moment.
- **Observe:** Acknowledge what is happening, whether it is good or bad, external or internal stimuli, and note it.
- **Proceed:** After briefly checking into the present moment, continue on with what was being done.

In the same way a student can use the acronym RAIN if they are struggling with feeling out of touch of the present moment:

- **Recognize:** Acknowledge what is happening, and note the significance of everything in a calm, accepting manner. This is a good time to use STOP to take a momentary pause.
- **Accept:** Know that life is just the way it is, without attempting to change it right away or wishing it were different.
- **Investigate:** See how what is being done feels. Is it creating feelings of being upset or happy, giving pleasure or pain? Note what you learn.
- **Non-identification:** Understand that the sensations that are being felt are for a fleeting experience that will soon pass. It does not define the present moment.

However mindfulness is implemented within the classroom, the act of creating an environment where students can take a break and reflect on their response to external and internal stimuli will change their whole mindset. Mindfulness meets individuals where they are at, and enables them to regulate their bodies and minds. Whether a student is on the playground, in the cafeteria, or in the middle of a test, mindfulness offers a way for the student to focus on how the body feels and create a sense of control in a situation that they feel is out of control.

READER TAKEAWAYS

- Mindfulness is the act of becoming more aware of the present by practicing skills such as deep breathing, meditation, or guided im-

agery in order to create a sense of stillness in an individual's body and mind.
- Mindfulness is especially important in children and adolescents because of the impact that it has on the executive functioning and healthy development of the brain.
- Mindfulness implemented within the classroom greatly influences the way the student learns, self-regulates, and interacts with peers and teachers.

REFERENCES

American Psychiatric Association. (2013). *Diagnostic and statistical manual of mental disorders* (5th ed.). Author.

Fan, Y., Tang, Y.-Y., Tang, R., & Posner, M. (2014). Short-term integrative meditation improves resting alpha activity and stroop performance. *Applied Psychophysiology and Biofeedback, 39*(3–4), 213–217.

Goldin, P. R., & Gross, J. J. (2010). Effects of Mindfulness-Based Stress Reduction (MBSR) on emotion regulation in social anxiety disorder, *10*(1), 83–91.

Kabat-Zinn, J., & Hanh, T. N. (2013). *Full catastrophe living: Using the wisdom of your body and mind to face stress, pain, and illness.* Bantam Books.

Schonert-Reichl, K. A., Oberle, E., Stewart Lawlor, M., Abbott, D., Thomson, K., Oberlander, T. F., & Diamond, A. (2015). Enhancing cognitive and social–emotional development through a simple-to-administer mindfulness-based school program for elementary school children: A randomized controlled trial. *Developmental Psychology, 51*(1), 52–66.

Teper, R., & Inzlicht, M. (2013). Meditation, mindfulness and executive control: The importance of emotional acceptance and brain-based performance monitoring. *Social Cognitive and Affective Neuroscience, 8*(1), 85–92.

Zelazo, P. D., Forston, J. L., Masten, A. S., & Carlson, S. M. (2018, February). Mindfulness plus reflection training: Effects on executive function in early childhood. *Frontiers in Psychology, 9*, 208. doi: 10.3389/fpsyg.2018.00208

About the Editors and Contributors

Anthony Avery, M.Ed., has been working in education for 16 years. During that time, his career has spanned private school to public education, from junior high to kindergarten, from special education to gifted students. Currently, Anthony works in instructional leadership in a large urban district in Texas. He has focused his professional development efforts throughout the years to help other educators better understand how to serve unique populations. His work has been centered around best instructional practices for special education students, literacy with an emphasis on writing for urban minority populations, and purposeful integration of instructional technology. One of the highlights of his career was the opportunity to teach English in Shanghai, China.

Kelly Binz has taught pre-kindergarten through eighth grade in Wisconsin and Texas. Her degree in special education has influenced her intentional use of strategies to increase student engagement. She is currently a fourth grade English and language arts teacher in Texas. As a mother of three, she values the unique personalities of each of her students. Her interests include mentoring student teachers and collaborating with peers to integrate games and play that support a pedagogy of care.

Lindsey Bird, M.Ed., has been in public education for 18 years in multiple capacities. As a high school social science instructor, developer and coordinator of an award-winning secondary newcomer program, and policy advocate for students new to the nation, she worked to expand opportunity and access to this subsection of the English learner demographic. She is currently a consultant, helping school districts identify policies and programs to better serve newcomer students and empowering classroom teachers with cultural competencies and instructional best practices.

Nita Brady is the founder and director of Beyond the Walls for Kids, a nonprofit program for children who have incarcerated family members.

She has worked extensively with families of inmates and incarcerated youth for more than 20 years. She is a speaker and an award-winning author. Several of her books have won the international Purple Dragonfly and the Royal Dragonfly Awards for Excellence in Children's Literature. She received the Soroptimist Club Ruby Award in 2013, and received the Stanislaus Partners in Education Award in 2019. She is a retired regional educator for a large hospital system, where she conducted staff development and leadership training for 21 years.

Heather Dean, Ph.D., has spent her career in education teaching English at the junior high and high school level. Currently, she is an assistant professor of teacher education at California State University, Stanislaus, with research interests in teacher retention, literacy education, and understanding best practices for training new teachers.

Jolleen de Clercq has served as an educator for 16 years. Her experience as a classroom teacher sparked a great awareness of the need to focus on students' emotional well-being, encouraging her to pursue and earn a master's degree in educational counseling and a pupil personnel services credential. Currently, she is an instructional coach for Ceres Unified School District in Ceres, California, collaborating with and supporting teachers to ensure achievement for all students.

Katherine Grayson, M.A., is a University of California, Berkeley, graduate and holds a master's degree in counseling psychology from John F. Kennedy University. With more than 20 years in business and nonprofit administration, she is currently the business manager at Without Permission.

Stephanie Heitkemper, M.A., has dedicated her career to companioning bereaved youth and their families. Currently, Stephanie is in private practice as a licensed professional counselor (LPC) and registered play therapist (RPT) in Colorado. She is recognized by the Association in Death Education and Counseling as a Fellow in Thanatology (FT).

Amelia Herrera, Ed.D., has been an educator of high school–aged immigrant, refugee, and asylum-seeking students for the last 14 years. Currently, she sits on the National Teacher Advisory Committee for Education Policy for Teach Plus. In addition, Amelia works with the California Department of Education to revise social-emotional education policy. She is also an adjunct professor of teacher education at California State University, Stanislaus. Her research interests include neuroscience, racialized trauma, Buddhism, trauma-informed care, and culturally responsive pedagogy.

Samantha Houston-Crook, M.S., is a registered associate marriage and family therapist (MFT) and registered associate professional clinical counselor (PCC) and has been working at a nonprofit as a school-based therapist. She has a background in cognitive psychology, counseling psychology, and mindfulness based stress reduction. Driven by further education and a desire for more in-depth work, Samantha is currently finishing her doctoral studies in trauma and disaster relief at Northcentral University.

Debbie Johnson is the founder and chief executive officer of the nonprofit organization Without Permission. A licensed minister since 2007 and a leader in the field of anti-human trafficking work for a decade, she spearheads the regional collaborative response to sex trafficking in California's Central Valley. Without Permission serves victims of sex trafficking and their families, and provides prevention education to school districts, law enforcement, and county agencies. Without Permission was awarded California District 12's Nonprofit of the Year in 2017. Debbie received the National FBI Director's Community Leadership Award, the Senate's Certificate of Recognition on the Status of Women, and recognition as a Woman of Distinction in Human Rights from the U.S. Congress.

Kourtney Kauffman, M.S., is a licensed marriage and family therapist (LMFT) and director of Family Concern Counseling, a division of Youth for Christ, Central Valley. She has worked for the past 12 years serving families, children, and adolescents, first as a case manager working with youth in foster care, and then as a therapist. She is a trainer and speaker, with specialties that include complex trauma, anxiety, and working with special populations such as foster and adoptive families and children as well as human trafficking survivors.

Nicole Lonergan, M.A., has taught secondary English for the last six years, both in private and public school settings. Currently, she teaches 10th grade English at Turlock High School in Turlock, California. In her teaching experience, Nicole has worked with honors students, college preparatory students, and students in a specialized program for high school sophomores deficient in credits. In addition to teaching, she runs the varsity girls soccer program at her high school. Nicole is currently finishing her master's degree in curriculum and instruction, focusing her research on writing self-efficacy of students and how to effectively use peer assessment in the classroom.

Ryan Lonergan, M.A., has been a secondary resource special education teacher for seven years and currently teaches at Johansen High School in Modesto, California. In his first year of teaching, Ryan also had the opportunity to work with a specialized program for students with emotional disturbances. In addition to teaching in the special education program, Ryan also taught a leadership class at his school for three years. He recently completed his master of arts in teaching leadership, where he focused his research on increasing special education students' self-advocacy skills in order to impact their academic progress. In addition to teaching, Ryan has run his school's varsity girls basketball program for the last three years, as well as coached boys and girls golf.

Nikkole Swanson, M.Ed., has been an educator for the past 16 years. Currently, she is serving as a K–8 literacy coach, specializing in early and adolescent literacy development. She has extensively researched and practiced strategies surrounding equity in education, culturally responsive teaching, and students with dyslexia. Nikkole received her master's degree in educational leadership from California State University, Stanislaus.

Samantha Van Horn, M.S., is a licensed marriage and family therapist (LMFT) and has spent much of her career providing clinical services to children and teens within the school setting. She is the school counseling services coordinator at Youth for Christ, Family Concern Counseling and is a certified clinical anxiety treatment professional. She is driven by interests in neurology, anxiety, trauma, human trafficking, children/teen developmental issues, and cultural issues.

Amber E. Wagnon, Ph.D., was a public school secondary educator for more than a decade. She is currently an assistant professor of secondary education at Stephen F. Austin State University where her research interests include literacy education, experiential learning, and public school advocacy.

Melissa Williams has been a classroom teacher for 10 years in kindergarten through fourth grade. She has served as a gifted and talented teacher, special education teacher, English as a Second Language campus specialist, and English and language arts interventionist. She researches, implements, and presents social and emotional learning strategies to staff and parents. Her 25 years of dance and theater experiences influence her interactive and energetic classroom. She currently teaches students with special needs at a public school in Texas.

www.ingramcontent.com/pod-product-compliance
Lightning Source LLC
Chambersburg PA
CBHW020125240426
43673CB00038B/595